DEVIL'S ADVOCATES

DEVIL'S ADVOCATES is a series of books devoted to exploring the classics of horror cinema. Contributors to the series come from the fields of teaching, academia, journalism and fiction, but all have one thing in common: a passion for the horror film and a desire to share it with the widest possible audience.

'The admirable Devil's Advocates series is not only essential – and fun – reading for the serious horror fan but should be set texts on any genre course.'
Dr Ian Hunter, Reader in Film Studies, De Montfort University, Leicester

'Auteur Publishing's new Devil's Advocates critiques on individual titles... offer bracingly fresh perspectives from passionate writers. The series will perfectly complement the BFI archive volumes.' **Christopher Fowler,** *Independent on Sunday*

'Devil's Advocates has proven itself more than capable of producing impassioned, intelligent analyses of genre cinema... quickly becoming the go-to guys for intelligent, easily digestible film criticism.' *Horror Talk.com*

'Auteur Publishing continue the good work of giving serious critical attention to significant horror films.' *Black Static*

 DevilsAdvocatesbooks

 DevilsAdBooks

T0311328

ALSO AVAILABLE IN THIS SERIES

Carrie Neil Mitchell

The Descent James Marriott

Halloween Murray Leeder

Let the Right One In Anne Billson

SAW Benjamin Poole

The Silence of the Lambs Barry Forshaw

The Texas Chain Saw Massacre James Rose

The Thing Jez Conolly

FORTHCOMING

Antichrist Amy Simmonds

Black Sunday Martyn Conterio

The Blair Witch Project Peter Turner

Near Dark John Berra

Nosferatu Cristina Massaccesi

Psychomania IQ Hunter & Jamie Sherry

DEVIL'S ADVOCATES

WITCHFINDER GENERAL

IAN COOPER

Acknowledgments

I'd like to thank John Atkinson at Auteur, who was encouraging about this book from the start and who has helped me immeasurably above and beyond the call of duty. I'd like to thank Kim Newman and Justin Smith for being good enough to provide me with useful materials. Also, my good friend Jackie Downs listened a lot and supplied me with ideas and reference material.

Although she has only managed to sit through Witchfinder General once, this book is for my wife, Julia Thaddey.

Ian Cooper, Neuss, March 2011

First published in 2011, reprinted in 2014 by
Auteur, 24 Hartwell Crescent, Leighton Buzzard LU7 1NP
www.auteur.co.uk
Copyright © Auteur 2011

Series design: Nikki Hamlett at Cassels Design
Set by Cassels Design www.casselsdesign.co.uk
Printed and bound by CPI Group (UK) Ltd, Croydon, CR0 4YY

Images from *Witchfinder General* taken from the Showbox Region 2 DVD © Tigon Films; *Cry of the Banshee* © AIP; *Blood on Satan's Claw* © Tigon Films; *Mark of the Devil* © Atlas International Film

British Library Cataloguing-in-Publication Data
A catalogue record for this book is available from the British Library

ISBN 978-1-906733-51-3
ebook ISBN: 978-1-906733-94-0

CONTENTS

Introduction 7

1. The Place of the Film 13

2. Context, Production and Reception 23

3. Analysis 57

4. The Influence of the Film 83

Bibliography 101

CONTENTS

INTRODUCTION

Witchfinder General (1968) was directed by Michael Reeves. A British/American co-production, it was financed by Tigon and American International Pictures. Based on the 1966 novel by Ronald Bassett, it stars Vincent Price as the title character with support from Ian Ogilvy, Hilary Dwyer, Rupert Davies and Robert Russell and cameo appearances from Patrick Wymark and Wilfred Brambell.

SYNOPSIS

The setting is England in 1645. It is the height of the Civil War and law and order have largely broken down. Taking opportunity of both the social upheaval and a superstitious populace, Matthew Hopkins, a lawyer turned witchfinder, travels through Suffolk and East Anglia with his brutish assistant John Stearne. Their mission is to extract confessions from those accused of witchcraft and mete out due punishment.

Richard Marshall is a soldier in Cromwell's army. After saving the life of his Captain, he is promoted to Cornet and given two days' leave. He travels to the village of Brandeston to be reunited with Sara, the woman he loves. She lives with her uncle, the clergyman John Lowes. Upon his arrival, Lowes tells Marshall he will consent to his marrying Sara on condition he takes her away from Brandeston. Sara and Marshall spend the night together. The next day, Marshall leaves to rejoin his platoon, stopping on the way to give directions to two men seeking Brandeston. Unbeknownst to the soldier, the men are Hopkins and Stearne and they are looking for Lowes, 'a man who may not be what he seems to be'.

Hopkins and Stearne confront Lowes and begin their examination, 'pricking' and 'running' him. When Sara arrives, Hopkins is attracted to her and she offers herself to save her Uncle. Hopkins orders Stearne to stop his examination and that night he has sex with Sara. The next night, Stearne follows Hopkins and learns of his arrangement with Sara. When Hopkins is called out to the next village, Stearne attacks and rapes Sara, an act witnessed by a villager. Upon his return, Hopkins is told of this and, in a jealous pique, he has the accused witches, including Lowes, 'swum' and hanged.

On patrol, Marshall is told by a horsetrader about Lowes' hanging and he rides to Brandeston. He finds Sara in the chapel, where they marry in the eyes of god and Marshall swears revenge. Before he leaves, he tells Sara to go to Lavenham where she should be safe. Marshall rejoins his platoon as three of his comrades are leaving to round up horses for the coming battle at Naseby. They encounter Hopkins and Stearne and while the witchfinder flees, Stearne is captured and his horse confiscated; but Stearne manages to kill his captors and escape.

After his victory at the Battle of Naseby, Oliver Cromwell asks to meet Cornet Marshall. He promotes him to Captain and asks him to travel to East Anglia to intercept the King, who may be trying to flee to the continent. Hopkins, meanwhile, has arrived in Lavenham, keen to try out a new method of execution. Stearne learns of Hopkins' whereabouts from a horsetrader and he sets off for Lavenham. Marshall's mission is unsuccessful but he, too, hears of the witchburning in Lavenham and rides there with his comrades.

In the village square, an accused witch is tied to a ladder and lowered into a fire. Stearne and Hopkins meet and they run into Sara. When Marshall arrives and goes to her lodgings, they are interrupted by the witchfinders, who accuse them and take them to a castle dungeon to seek a confession.

Stearne's torture of Sara is interrupted by the arrival of Marshall's comrades. Marshall breaks free and stamps on Stearne's face, knocking out an eye before attacking Hopkins with an axe, hacking at him repeatedly. When his comrades arrive, they are horrified at the carnage and one of them shoots the mutilated Hopkins. The furious Richard mutters 'You took him from me' over and over again until it turns into a shout as the hysterical Sara starts to scream.

A DISREPUTABLE CLASSIC

Witchfinder General occupies a unique place in British cinema. On the one hand, it is frequently cited as a landmark film, well-regarded, influential and critically acclaimed. In 1995, it appeared in the BBC 100 film list compiled to mark a century of cinema and 'The Guardian' critic, Derek Malcolm, included it in his 'Century of Films', describing it as 'one of the most compulsively watchable ever made in Britain' (2000). The critic Robin Wood was an admirer of the film: 'what one is immediately struck by is the assurance and intensity of what is on the screen' (1969: 2) and for Mark Kermode it is 'widely regarded as the single most significant horror film produced in the UK in the 1960s' (2002:14). Julian Petley describes it as 'one of the towering achievements, not simply of British horror but of British cinema *tout court*' (1986: 100) while David Pirie, in his seminal study of British gothic cinema, 'A Heritage of Horror', states that Reeves' film:

> generates a power which scarcely diminishes upon repeated viewing... *Witchfinder General* is unlike anything else that was being done at the time and (regrettably) has been done since. (2009:167)

He goes on to suggest it 'brings UK horror to some kind of maturity' (2009: 175) and compares director Michael Reeves to the poet John Keats. The Keats comparison arises in no small part due to the untimely death of the director from a barbiturate overdose at the age of 25, only months after the release of *Witchfinder*.

However, for many critics, it remains a disreputable work with a troubled history. Even the title is disputed, the film being also known as *Witchfinder-General*, *The Conqueror Worm* and *Edgar Allan Poe's The Conqueror Worm*, with Kim Newman arguing for *Matthew Hopkins Witchfinder General*, after the on-screen title credit (see Newman 1988: 2003). The film was heavily cut in the UK and re-titled and later re-scored in the USA. In Europe, it was spiced-up with extraneous scenes of cavorting topless wenches. Upon its initial release, it was regarded by many as an exercise in sadism that heralded the ultra-violence of 1970s cinema. The playwright and critic Alan Bennett called the film 'the most persistently sadistic and rotten film I have seen', adding, for good measure, 'there are no laughs in 'Witchfinder General' (in Murray 2002: 263) For Dilys Powell it was 'peculiarly nauseating' (in Murray 2002: 262) Only Michael Powell's *Peeping Tom* (1960), a work similarly praised and vilified, occupies a similar space in British national film culture.

However, both *Witchfinder General* and its doomed young director continue to resonate, being frequently discussed, studied and referenced. 2002 saw the publication of John B. Murray's oral history 'The Remarkable Michael Reeves', sub-titled 'His Short and Tragic Life' while the critical biography, 'Michael Reeves' by Benjamin Halligan was published the following year. On the 20th February 2003, a 'black plaque' for the director was unveiled by the organisation English Heretic, at Ipswich Cemetery, where the director's ashes were scattered exactly 34 years before.

The plaque is one of a series designed to:

commemorate and draw public attention to historical figures in such diverse fields as sorcery, the Royal Art, left-hand path esotericism and witchcraft as well as the mentally infirm: tortured poets, anti-heroes and village idiots. (undated)

2003 was also the year that *Witchfinder General* was added to the AS Level Film Studies syllabus in the UK as a 'Focus Film' for British Cinema (replacing that other cult favourite, *The Wicker Man* [1973]) and Prism Video released the film on R2 DVD in a 'Special Edition' that included previously-censored footage. In 2005, Total Film magazine voted *Witchfinder General* the 15th 'greatest horror film of all time' (*The Texas Chainsaw Massacre* was at number one). In September 2007, after some prolonged lobbying by fans, Sony released a remastered R1 DVD, restoring censored footage and the evocative score by Paul Ferris.

October 2007 saw a Magic Lantern show, *Michael Reeves Directs*, performed at the Horse Hosptial in London by artist Mark Ferreli, where 'projected images, spoken word, and ambient sound' are used to 'summon the still resonant voice of the young director' (undated). The second half of 2008 saw a flurry of screenings and related activity. September saw the 'Reel History' feature in 'The Guardian' damn the film with faint praise:

bearing in mind 'Witchfinder General' is a cheap schlocky horror film, it manages to be a remarkably accurate piece of historical film-making. (von Tunzelmann 2008)

The same month also saw the most recent screening of the film to date at London's National Film Theatre, with an introduction by the critic Julian Petley. In 'The Independent' newspaper of 14th November 2008, *Witchfinder General* is discussed in relation to a forthcoming TV drama, *The Devil's Whore* and the ARTE TV Channel in Germany screened the European version, *Der Hexenjäger*, later that same month as part of its 'Arte Trash' strand. Reeves' earlier film, *The Sorcerers* was also part of this disparate season of weird cinema along with the LSD movie *The Trip* (1967) and *Glen or Glenda* (1953) by Ed Wood.

In 2009, Michael Reeves' little-seen debut *La Sorellla Di Satani* (1965) was given its first official DVD release from Dark Sky under one of its many titles, *The She-Beast*. The *Witchfinder General* page on the social networking site Facebook was started in June 2009. (As of January 2011 it has 920 fans.) The whole film was uploaded to the video-sharing site Youtube in 2009, along with a number of related videos. These include the Matthew Hopkins story told in animated woodcuts and home-made music videos for the 'Love Theme from *Witchfinder General*' by the Roberto Mann Orchestra and the oddball Carl Douglas track, 'Witchfinder General', which includes lyrics such as:

> Witchfinder General gives everyone a fright,
> Witchfinder General this man is really out of sight,
> Says he's got a thing about burning witches,
> Some of these were mighty fine bitches.

In March 2010, the Radio 4 Saturday Play was 'Vincent Price and the Horror of the English Blood-Beast' by Matthew Broughton, which played the supposed animosity between director Reeves and star Price for laughs.

Despite its exploitation roots, then, *Witchfinder General* has proved to be a resonant and influential piece of work, a still-startling slice of home-grown gothic. This study will attempt to explain why.

CHAPTER 1. THE PLACE OF THE FILM

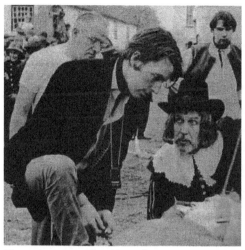

Witchfinder General is not notable solely due to its strange status as 'a disreputable classic'. It also draws on a number of British and American popular forms (such as the costume melodrama, the horror film and the Western). It is also a striking example of an auteur sensibility in what Robin Wood calls 'that most discouraging of areas – the British commercial cinema' (1969: 7).

Director Reeves consulting with star Price

Vincent Price: 'I've made 84 films. How many have you made?'

Michael Reeves: 'Three good ones'.

This oft-quoted, possibly apocryphal, on-set exchange between star and director is a good illustration of Reeves' precocity and self-confidence. A significant 'Cult of Personality' has arisen around the director since his early death at the age of 25.

Inevitably, there have been many comparisons with other precocious *wunderkinder*. Bill Kelley dubbed him 'the James Dean of horror' (1991) and for producer Paul Maslansky, he was an 'English Spielberg' (1999) while 'The Village Voice' settled for 'the most audacious visual talent to have come out of England since Hitchcock' (in Murray 2002).

In many ways, the director is the archetypal tortured artist. Male, handsome if a bit geeky, single-minded, prone to self-medication and dying young in faintly mysterious circumstances, leaving an impressive, if slim, body of work and an awful lot of 'what ifs?'

Peter John Dyer, reviewing Carlos Claren's book 'Horror Movies' for 'Sight and Sound' in 1968 noted:

the aura of sadness that haunts so many horror films, their makers and performers. Yet think of Méliès, the Wizard of Montreuil, dying in a Home for the Destitute...think of the mysterious deaths of Murnau and James Whale; the tragic elements in the deaths of Lon Chaney Snr., Laird Cregar, Peter Lorre, Warner Oland (the lycanthrope Yogami in *Werewolf of London*) and Sybille Schmitz, the beautiful Leone of Dreyer's *Vampyr* who committed suicide in 1955. Think especially of the inimitable Bela Lugosi. (1968: 212)

(And one could extend Dyer's thesis, adding names such as director Paul Leni, actors Colin Clive and Dwight Frye, directors Anthony Balch and William Girdler as well as the *Witchfinder* cinematographer John Coquillon who may have killed himself aged 57 and composer Paul Ferris who took a fatal overdose aged 54.)

As Pirie (2009) notes, only a matter of weeks after Dyer's article was published, Reeves was found dead on the floor of his bedroom, having taken an overdose of barbiturates.

The director was by, any measure, an intensely troubled man. He had been receiving treatment for depression and anxiety, was drinking a lot and was prescribed medication (including the sedatives that were to kill him). Nicky Henson, actor and friend of the director, told John Murray how 'he had pills to sleep, pills to get up, uppers and downers. On prescription from the doctor. He lived his life through those pills' (2002: 316). The writer and chronicler of London Iain Sinclair also knew Reeves: 'he was using a lot of pills: Valium, lithium, barbiturates' (1997: 296).

He had been hospitalised and at one stage was even given electroconvulsive therapy. In the months before he died, his mental state deteriorating, he broke up with his girlfriend and moved from his mews cottage in Knightsbridge to a flat in Chelsea. Sinclair illustrates this change (both geographical and mental) with an apt film reference, suggesting the director 'was drifting into the climate of the last reel of *The Servant*' (Ibid.), invoking Joseph Losey's disturbing tale of mental disintegration.

A number of sources have, over the years, suggested Reeves' death was suicide (including, on occasion, Vincent Price and *Witchfinder* composer Paul Ferris, who told Murray, 'Mike wanted to die, I know' [2002: 316]). However, the Coroner recorded a verdict of accidental death and the amount of drugs in his system was found to be 'consistent with an injudicious overdosage rather than an attempt to commit suicide' (in Murray 2002: 324).

But given the tragic, vaguely mysterious nature of his early death, it's no wonder that the director's personal problems and precarious mental state are often referred to in discussions of his films. Reeves has become one of those artists whose work is coloured, perhaps even framed by their premature deaths (this far-from-select group includes Rudolph Valentino, Sylvia Plath, Rainer Werner Fassbinder and Kurt Cobain).

Peter Hutchings has written of the 'all-encompassing nihilistic despair' in *Witchfinder* as well as an ending which suggests 'an inability to go further, to put something else, something more positive in its stead' (1993: 150-1). Hutchings' analysis of the *Witchfinder General* credit sequence is useful in this context. He identifies 'an assertion of a particular mystificatory notion of authorship' (1993: 146) in the parade of lithographs (all images from elsewhere in the film).

> This credit sequence consists of distorted, grainy photographs of various individuals, male and female, suffering and in pain (with one image of Stearne, the witchfinder's assitant, laughing). The final image shown is that of a human face – it is difficult to say whether it is male or female – contorted into a scream. Over this face appears Michael Reeves' directorial credit. The statement thereby implied could not be clearer. The artist is in despair, a despair which is existential, outside history, ungendered, beyond analysis. (Hutchings 1993: 146-7)

Robin Wood saw signs in Reeves' work of 'a painful hypersensitivity in its creator' (1969: 5). Tim Lucas sums up this connection between the man and the work well:

> The news of his death resonated apace with the climactic scream of his third and final feature...Just as *Witchfinder's* cynicism went on to make downbeat endings *de rigeur* in the horror genre for years to follow, so its romanticism attached itself to the young director's thwarted promise...the impact of Reeves' death remained a compelling point of attraction for a certain breed of film fan. Almost ten years ago, I found myself consoling the widow of someone who committed suicide not long after acquiring a bust of Michael Reeves; it fell to me to explain to her who he was. (2009: 88)

As well as Reeves' posthumous casting as the angst king of British horror, there has been and continues to be considerable speculation about what he may have gone on to achieve. Although ultimately pointless, this is also hard to avoid. It is tempting to think about what Reeves may have come up with had his career developed over decades, particularly if one accepts Robin Woods' assertion that:

> Reeves' death is a tragic loss for British cinema, the more so in that none of his films is completely satisfactory, that one is aware of more promise than achievement. (1969: 6)

The most entertaining (and poignant) speculation is contained in 'What If?: Michael Reeves', an on-line essay by David N. from 2007 which sketches out a shadow life for the director wherein, as well as acquiring then kicking a heroin habit and marrying Blaxploitation star Vonetta McGee, he films adaptations of novels such as 'The Man in the High Castle' by Phillip K. Dick and Theodor Roszak's 'Flicker'.

The truth is, if we put such speculative fantasies to one side and judge Reeves solely on what he did achieve in his short life, he remains a filmmaker of considerable power, whose filmography consists of (in his own words) 'three good ones'.

LEE, STEELE AND KARLOFF

Michael Leith Reeves was born into a wealthy family and 'decided to make films when he was eight' (Tom Baker, quoted in 1999). As a teenager, he made films on 8 and 16mm, mounting the camera on his mother's tea-tray for tracking shots. His shorts, *Carrion* (1958) and *Intrusion* (1961) already bear his authorial stamp, being violent genre pieces featuring Ian Ogilvy. Benjamin Halligan (2003) has written convincingly of how the latter film (which has recently resurfaced and can be seen in a slightly-abbreviated form on Youtube) foreshadows *Witchfinder* thematically and visually: both films open with shots of tree branches and use a rural setting as a backdrop for brutality.

In 1963, after inheriting a considerable sum of money, he travelled to America and introduced himself to the American genre director Don Siegel. Accounts of their first meeting differ, but in all of them Reeves acknowledges the older man as 'the greatest film director in the world'. After working as dialogue director on some of Siegel's test shoots, Reeves used this experience to get bits of work, including acting as 'gofer' on the Richard Widmark viking movie, *The Long Ships* (1963).

In 1964, he did some work in a still-disputed capacity on an Italian horror film, *Il castello dei morti vivi / Castle of the Living Dead* (1964) starring Christopher Lee and a then-unknown Canadian actor, Donald Sutherland (in no less than three roles). There is still considerable confusion over Reeves' role in the production. Although the film is the work of an American, Warren Kiefer, various prints credit Italian directors including Lorenzo Sabatini and Luciano Ricci. These credits were apparently added for tax and quota purposes but the confusion remains: the Internet Movie Database (IMDb), for example, credits Keifer, Sabatini and Ricci. Robin Wood is one of a number of critics who identify some Reevesian authorial touches in the film, including the use of a 'Bergmanesque dwarf'. But the most authoritative source would seem to be Halligan who suggests Kiefer was indeed the main creative force on the picture, with Reeves overseeing some shots 'but nothing that would ultimately make for any discernable authorial imprint on the film' (2003: 41).

In 1965 he directed his first solo feature, *La Sorella di Satani / Revenge of the Blood Beast* aka *The She-Beast*, another Italian production. The film stars Barbara Steele, the iconic British star of Italian horror (who worked for one very long day) and alongside her, Reeves' friend, Ogilvy, who would go on to star in all of the director's subsequent films. It's the very generic story of a young couple honeymooning in Transylvania who unwittingly unleash the vengeful spirit of the titular beast, an executed witch called Vardella.

The film is certainly harmed by its micro-budget (the cinematography and the sound are terrible) and a lot of the jokes fall flat. But it's often strikingly composed and directed with some flair, as in the oft-remarked upon scene where the witch attacks a man with a sickle before tossing it away, only for it to land across a hammer (geddit?) The powerful opening scene has been described by Robin Wood as evoking 'comparison with the nightmare visions of Hieronymus Bosch' (1969: 3), as the hideously ugly Vardella is dragged from her cave to a lake, impaled on a red-hot spike and drowned on a ducking stool. This opening prefigures the opening of *Witchfinder*, even down to some of the camera placements. We see the torch-wielding mob silhouetted against trees, with the sound of the wind blowing; a shot from behind the ducking stool, showing the mob with their bound captive, getting nearer, the ducking stool torture, being watched by a priest and a crowd of silent, impassive villagers.

This short sequence also effectively conveys the recurring themes of violence, degradation and contagious evil, themes that were to reach fruition in *Witchfinder General*. As Wood puts it:

> the vileness of the witch is matched by the horror of what is being done to her: victim and destroyers are reduced to a common bestiality. Or, if you like, Vardella's viciousness is felt as being reflected in the righteous who surround her, an ineffaceable universal principle. (Ibid.)

Sadly, budgetary constraints put paid to the proposed ending, which was to take place in London, with the husband having sex with his beautiful wife only to see her turn into Vardella. This planned ending is interesting in the light of the 'downer' endings of Reeves' other, more accomplished, films.

His British debut was *The Sorcerers* (1967). As with *Witchfinder General*, the star of the film is an iconic genre figure: in this case, Boris Karloff. It's a low-key science fiction film, based on a novel by John Burke and scripted by Reeves and Tom Baker, an old friend of the director, who had graduated from operating the camera on *Intrusion* and would go on to co-write the *Witchfinder General* screenplay. *The Sorcerers* is a stylish, atmospheric story about an aged inventor, Professor Montserrat (Karloff) and his cruel reptilian wife (Catherine Lacey) who use an experimental mind control device on a hip, alienated young antique-dealer (!) Mike Roscoe (Ogilvy), enabling them to experience vicariously all of the sensations he experiences. These experiences include midnight swimming, motorcyling and murder. Clearly an allegory of the cinematic experience, it also casts a very jaundiced eye on the 'Swinging London' scene. The mind control sequence, with its coloured gels, flickering strobes and atonal electronic whining is clearly intended to evoke the contemporary psychedelic 'happenings'. Montserrat comes over as a malign version of acid guru Timothy Leary, offering not liberation but submission. He prepares Roscoe for the experiment by telling him to 'relax, clear your mind, empty your mind of all thoughts' – words that recall The Beatles song, 'Tomorrow Never Knows' with its 'switch off your mind, relax and float downstream' (itself inspired by a book co-written by Leary).

As Halligan says of Montserrat's hypnotic lightshows:

> rather than opening up the mind, they work to shut it down – control rather than
> freedom, blackouts rather than hallucinations; a trap not a trip. (2003: 76)

Elsewhere, Roscoe sneers at a club full of would-be hipsters 'How long do you think all this can last?' *The Sorcerers'* twin themes of pessimism and exploitation of the young by immoral, corrupt elders were to re-surface in *Witchfinder General*.

Reeves was obsessed with films: Paul Ferris, who composed the score for *Witchfinder*, describes him as '*movie mad*. It was his life, thoughts, dreams, the lot' (in Murray 202: 99, emphasis in original). Of course, post-Scorsese, post-Tarantino, the template of the geeky male obsessed with cinematic detritus is a familiar one. But by 1960s standards, Reeves brand of cinephilia was strikingly unusual, manifested in an obsession with a select number of disparate genre films. These include works by Roger Corman, Ralph Nelson (*Duel at Diablo* [1966]) and Michael Winner (*I'll Never Forget Whats'isname* [1968]).

Reeves' love of mainstream, Anglophone cinema went hand-in-hand with a rejection of the then-voguish European art cinema, perhaps best summed up in his lionisation of action film specialist Don Siegel at the expense of contemporary iconic figures such as Federico Fellini, Sergio Leone and François Truffaut. Screenwriter Tom Baker recalls Reeves rejecting trips to see arthouse films with 'Oh Christ, I'm not going to read sub-titles all night, I don't want to see this stuff' (quoted in Murray 2002: 100-1). Reeves' short, *Intrusion,* does begin with a dedication to Jean-Luc Godard but this may be ironic: the film owes much more to Siegel than to the iconoclastic French director.

As well as Siegel (whose importance is discussed further in Chapter 3), Reeves also seems to have been influenced by action auteurs Sam Fuller and Robert Aldrich. Their 'tough guy' genre films would often tip over into hysteria, excess and sadism, what Andrew Sarris calls 'demonic distortions' (They Shoot Pictures, Don't They?): Fuller's *Shock Corridor* (1963) and *The Naked Kiss* (1964), for example, or Aldrich's *Whatever Happened to Baby Jane?* (1962) and *The Legend of Lylah Clare* (1968). Like Siegel, Fuller and Aldrich made stripped-down, violent films, thrillers, war films, Westerns. Certainly the pace, energy and pessimism of *Witchfinder* suggests the influence of American genre films rather than the stately studio-bound gothic of Terence Fisher and Mario Bava.

Indeed, David Pirie contrasts Reeves' approach to film with that of the Hammer director Fisher, who worked as a writer and editor until turning director aged 44. Fisher and his contemporaries would, in Pirie's words,

> have considered it highly eccentric to become passionately involved in the contemporary popular film scene as avid spectator/critics. To them, the craft of films was learned, not in cinemas, but in the cutting-rooms and the studios. Reeves, however, was only the first of a number of young writer/directors who now entered British horror movies with a long apprenticeship as voracious cinéastes. (2009: 168)

Perhaps the best way to understand Michael Reeves is to regard him as a home-grown 'Movie Brat'. This was the name given to the geeky American cinephiles who were inspired by the critics-turned-directors of the French New Wave such as Truffaut and Godard. These film-school-educated 'Brats', who included such luminaries as Martin Scorsese, Francis Ford Coppola, George Lucas and Brian De Palma, would make a number of innovative genre films which were to revolutionise Hollywood in the 1970s and beyond.

Tim Lucas has accurately described Reeves as:

> a remarkable autodidact who learned more from watching films obsessively and independently than his most talented film-school peers – Coppola, Bogdanovich, De Palma and Spielberg – were capable of putting onscreen during his lifetime. (2009: 88)

Indeed, like Coppola, Scorsese and Peter Bogdanovich, Reeves was drawn to the 'King of the Bs' Roger Corman. One of the projects Reeves was considering at the time of his death was the AIP gangster movie *Bloody Mama* (1970), which ended up being directed by Corman.

It may be that his depressive illness and his intense, obsessive cinephilia were in some way connected or that they at least complemented each other. David Thomson, in his article 'Dark, depressive, volatile - the film buff who lost the plot' argues that the seductive fantasy-world of film may be 'especially beguiling to those who live near the edge of gloom or self-destruction' (2004). Thomson was writing about Jerry Harvey, the charismatic screenwriter and cable channel film programmer who killed his wife before shooting himself (with a gun given to him by the film-maker Sam Peckinpah, whose connections to Reeves will be examined in Chapter 3).[1] However, Thomson's comments can be applied just as well to the director of *Witchfinder General*:

> Maybe the obsession is too great and too dark. Maybe it beckons too powerfully to the self-destructive, or the fantasist...People go into film as if it is a consuming country...there are unhappy, unsettled souls, much moved by the romance of film and much endangered by it...You never quite realise that film can be an empire that excludes you from real life until you look around in the necessary darkness and realise that the exits have gone. (2004)

Or as a character in *Peeping Tom* puts it – 'all this filming, it's not healthy'.

FOOTNOTES

[1] The story of Jerry Harvey is told in the documentary feature *Z Channel: A Magnificent Obsession* (2004), directed by Xan Cassavetes.

Chapter 2. Context, Production and Reception

The Man

In 1563, the Witchcraft Act came into force in Scotland and England. During the reign of James I, the Witchcraft Statute of 1604 decreed it a more serious crime, punishable by hanging. Matthew or Mathew Hopkins (ca. 1620–47) was a witch-hunter during the English Civil War who bestowed upon himself the title of Witchfinder General. He was the son of a clergyman from Grantham, Lincolnshire, although some accounts (including Bassett's novel) claim he was born in Wenham, Suffolk. Hopkins was widely believed to have trained as a lawyer (indeed, most accounts still describe him as such) although there is no conclusive proof of this. He was active from 1645–7 in the East of England including East Anglia, Suffolk, Norfolk and Essex.

With his assistant John Stearne, Hopkins condemned and executed 230 suspected witches, 'more than all the other witch-hunters that proliferated during the 160-year peak of the country's witchcraft hysteria' (Knowles 2007). Hopkins made a comfortable living as a witchfinder, being paid 20 shillings for every unfortunate found guiilty (at a time when the average daily wage was less than 3 pence). He used a number of methods to expose the accused. These included examining the body for 'teats' (in reality, warts or moles) used to suckle familiars such as black cats and 'pricking', whereby a 'bodkin' (a long needle) was used to prick the teats, on the basis that a witch wouldn't bleed. Hopkins took no chances with the latter test, using a bodkin with a retractable point. Additional methods included sleep-deprivation and 'swimming' or 'ducking' where the accused would be lowered into water: floating was a sign that the water rejected them and this was proof of witchcraft. Needless to say, drowning was proof of innocence.

Contrary to the impression given in the film, Hopkins did not serve as judge, jury and executioner. He would seek a confession to be used during an examination by magistrates. The purpose of this examination was to decide if the accused should be remanded for trial. Many of the details of the confessions would be amusing in any other context. For example, Elizabeth Clarke, an elderly one-legged woman whose mother had been hanged as a witch, apparently confessed to having:

> kept and nourished five familiars, Holt – a white kitten, Jarmara – a fat spaniel, Sack and Sugar – a black rabbit, Newes – a polecat and Vinegar Tom - a long legged greyhound with a head like an ox, broad eyes and a long tail. (Knowles 2007)

Later investigations threw up familiars named Elemanzer, Pyewacket, Peck in the Crown and Grizzel Greedigut, leading Hopkins to suggest these were 'names that no mortal could invent' (Knowles 2007). Of course, this witch-craze was not simply a result of ignorance and social breakdown. It was also a way to settle scores with old enemies: as one character in Bassett's novel puts it:

> Aye – if ye've a spiteful neighbour, an ugly wife, a rude landlord, a long-dying aunt or a threatening creditor – ye'll find the witchfinder'll take a nod or a wink and ye'll not be troubled after, so long as ye keep a quiet tongue in ye're head. (1966: 131)

In 1647, Hopkins' book 'The Discovery of Witches' was published, detailing his activities and aiming to dispell persistent rumours that he himself was in league with Satan. It begins with the Biblical quote, 'Thou shalt not suffer a witch to live' (Exodus 22:18).

Although there are accounts of Hopkins being hanged as a witch (after being 'swum' by a mob of angry villagers), the reality is more prosaic. He died in his bed of an illness, more than likely consumption.

THE NOVEL

> Vicious, tireless, Matthew Hopkins the Witchfinder General, scourge of the ungodly, flayer of the demented, burst into 1645 like a black-winged merciless Attila, leaving behind him a trail of gibbet-hung corpses and vermin-infested gaols filled with beaten, terrified women – like bloody footprints across the length of Suffolk. (Bassett 1966: 139)

In 1966, Ronald Bassett's novel 'Witchfinder General' was published. The book is dismissed by many who write about the film: Benjamin Halligan, for example, calls it 'tedious low-brow popular history' (2003: 106) while Andy Boot calls it 'turgid' (1999:

183). *Witchfinder's* co-screenwriter Tom Baker is more measured, saying 'I read the book. I don't like it very much, but then I'm not particularly into violence' (in Murray 2002: 160).

It's certainly densely-written and exposition-heavy but it's also an exciting treatment of the Hopkins story. Bassett largely sticks to the (few) known facts, with some interesting deviations. For example, as the novel begins, Hopkins is fighting in the Parliamentary army. He is described as 'shabby' and can't even afford a horse. He and Stearne have a henchwoman, the revolting Goody Phillips, who searches female suspects for teats. Later, Hopkins is press-ganged into fighting at the Battle of Naseby before being robbed of his savings by Stearne. The Marshall character is called Margery and he has a child with Sara, while Cromwell makes a couple of appearances, not only meeting Margery but also Hopkins.

Bassett's Hopkins is calculating, greedy and murderous but he also firmly believes in witches. While supervising his first interrogation, he seems convinced when told that the suspect's five familiars have put in an appearance, running into the cell and molesting her interrogator. The climax of the novel reworks the popular version of Hopkins' demise, as Margery and his men 'swim' the witchfinder before hanging him.

Even before Bassett's novel was published, Tony Tenser, the owner of Tigon Films, had bought the film rights, describing it as having 'some scope to it, some breadth to it' (quoted in Murray 2002: 159).

TIGON

Tony Tenser is one of the most important figures in the history of British horror cinema. Screenwriter and author David McGillivray suggested in 1992 that:

> The British film industry is gasping its last because there is no one like Tony Tenser to kick it back to life. He was the Irving Thalberg of the exploitation movie and, like the boy wonder of MGM, his career was too short. (in Sweet 2005: 264)

Tenser had impeccable credentials for a career in exploitation. After working as a publicist (where he coined the phrase 'sex kitten' for Brigitte Bardot), Tenser formed

Compton Films with strip-club owner, Michael Klinger. As well as 'nudie' movies such as *Naked...as Nature Intended* (1961) Compton also produced Roman Polanski's first English-language films, *Repulsion* (1965) and *Cul-de-Sac* (1966). For Matthew Sweet, Tenser's dealing with (comparative) newcomers like Polanski and Reeves exemplify 'his most cherishable quality: his willingness to take a chance on untested talents' (2005: 267). The critical and commercial success of the Polanski films conferred a kind of respectability on Tenser, who spilt with Klinger in 1966 and formed Tigon Films, aka Tigon British Film Productions, that same year.

Until they folded in 1972, Tigon produced a number of interesting projects such as the cod-psychedelia of *Curse of the Crimson Altar* (1968), the Raquel Welch rape-revenge Western *Hannie Caulder* (1971) and the *Witchfinder*-influenced *Blood on Satan's Claw* (1970). They also made the woeful Norman Wisdom sex comedy *What's Good for the Goose* (1969) and *The Blood Beast Terror* (1967) about a Victorian doctor's daughter who turns into a giant flesh-eating moth. Reeves' first British feature, *The Sorcerers*, was a Tigon production and Tenser seems to have regarded the director as a young auteur in the Polanski mould, signing him to a five year/five film contract. Aware that a period film shot on location would cost more than Tigon's usual fare, Tenser approached American International Pictures with a co-production offer.

AMERICAN INTERNATIONAL PICTURES (AIP)

AIP was started in 1956 by James H. Nicholson and Samuel Z. Arkoff. From the outset, they specialised in the production and distribution of low-budget projects targeted at the newly-emergent teenage audience. This meant lurid titles (such as *The Brain Eaters* [1958] and *How to Stuff a Wild Bikini* [1965]) and a reliance on genres: principally horror and sci-fi but also race-car, 'juvenile delinquent' and beach party films. Always keen to exploit trends, AIP would adjust their product with the times, so as the *zeitgeist* shifted from giant radioactive bugs and drag-racing to LSD and motorcycles, the company came up with the likes of *The Trip* (1967) and *Hell's Angels on Wheels* (1967).

AIP's best-known producer-director was the aforementioned Roger Corman. Corman was not just a talented (if consistently under-rated) filmmaker but also remarkably productive (making seven films in one year and shooting *The Terror* [1963] in a weekend) with a remarkable eye for talent-spotting: his discoveries include Jack Nicholson, Martin Scorsese, Jonathan Demme, Robert DeNiro and James Cameron.

Corman directed a number of cult classics, including *Bucket of Blood* (1959), *Little Shop of Horrors* (1960), *The Wild Angels* (1966) and *The St. Valentine's Day Massacre* (1967) as well as the memorably-titled *Teenage Cave Man* (1958), *The Saga of the Viking Women and their Voyage to the Waters of the Great Sea Serpent* (1957) and *Gas! Or It Became Necessary To Destroy the World In Order To Save It* (1970). But Corman's best-known works are the series of Edgar Allan Poe adaptations he made for AIP.

These eight films, from *The Fall of the House of Usher* (1960) to *The Tomb of Ligeia* (1965) although frequently owing little to their source material except a title, are a striking achievement, belying their B-movie status with lush settings, rich colour photography and witty, literate scripts. Their camp self-mocking humour, lurid plots and hallucinatory, psychedelic touches caught the mood of the times and appealed to the cine-literate youth crowd: Tony Rayns has written of the 'secret kinship' that exists between Corman's gothic horrors and the counter-culture (2006: 179).

Although they utilised a number of genre stalwarts, including Karloff, Barbara Steele, Peter Lorre and Basil Rathbone, the Poe films are most closely associated with Vincent Price, who starred in seven of the eight pictures. His star presence, with that sonorous, much-impersonated voice and stylised acting, was to the Poe series what Peter Cushing and Christopher Lee were to Hammer, and his work for Corman would help make Price a genre icon.

THE PRICE OF FEAR

Vincent Price was born in St. Louis, Missouri in 1911. He studied art history at Yale and attended The Courtauld Institute in London before becoming an actor. He had memorable roles in the films noir *Laura* (1944) and *Leave Her to Heaven* (1945) and his role as the sinister anti-hero in *Dragonwyck* (1946) foreshadows the autocratic gothic persona he would adopt in the latter part of his career. In the 1950s, he appeared in a number of hit horror films, including the 3-D *House of Wax* (1953) and *The Fly* (1958).

He was nearly 50 when he appeared in *The Fall of the House of Usher* and this led to his reinvention as a cult horror star, his playing style a well-judged mixture of the sinister and the camp.

Reeves' film was one of a number of films Price made in Britain in the late sixties and early seventies. Others include another Don Siegel-inspired project, *Scream and Scream Again* (1969) and a couple of AIP films, *The Oblong Box* (1969) and the *Witchfinder* rip-off *Cry of the Banshee* (1970). He also took on a number of roles that explicitly 'foreground acting and performance thematically' (Hunt 1996: 126), including *The Abominable Dr. Phibes* (1971) and *Theatre of Blood* (1973), which lace their gory revenge narratives with lots of black humour. He also provided sepulchral voice-overs for recordings by Alice Cooper and Michael Jackson. One of his last roles before his death in 1993 was as the creator/father of *Edward Scissorhands* (1990) directed by long-time admirer Tim Burton.

AIP accepted Tenser's co-production offer and put up half of the film's £100, 000 budget, seeing the film as a potential tax write-off which nevertheless would see them move into the booming British horror market.

BRITISH GOTHIC: THE X-CERTIFICATE, COLOUR AND CLEAVAGE

It certainly seems to be arguable on commercial, historical and artistic grounds that the horror genre, as it has been developed in this country by Hammer and its rivals, remains the only staple cinematic myth which Britain can properly claim its own, and which relates to it in the same way as the western relates to America. (Pirie 2009: xv)

Although horror would, in time, become a key part of British film culture, it took a while. Julian Petley has pointed out the irony that the country that spawned Mary Shelley, Lord Byron, Bram Stoker and a number of other exponents of fantastic and horrific literature should be so 'peculiarly slow in developing the horror film and the whole area of fantasy cinema' (1986: 113). It was only when a small production company called Hammer released a series of lurid, Eastmancolour gothics in the 1950s, that the genre became fully established in the UK. The reasons it took so long were many and varied.

Perhaps the chief reason for this slow start is a long-standing British prejudice against fantasy, in favour of a marked preference for the prosiac and the naturalistic, what David Pirie calls 'the tyranny of realism' (2009: 10). In his influential 1986 essay, 'The Lost Continent', Julian Petley rails against the dominance of the realist aesthetic:

> Of course, the vaunting and valorisation of of certain British films on account of their 'realism' entails, as its corollary, as the other side of the coin, the dismissal and denigration of those films deemed un-or non-realist. (1986: 98)

For Petley, the output of studios such as Gainsborough and Hammer and the work of directors such as the American expatriate Joseph Losey, Michael Powell and Reeves:

> form an other repressed side of British cinema, a dark disdained thread weaving the length and breadth of that cinema, crossing authorial and generic boundaries, sometimes almost entirely invisible, sometimes erupting explosively, always received critically with fear and disapproval. (Ibid.)

Both Pirie and Petley cite shocking examples of the wilful ignorance certain directors have expressed towards this 'dark disdained' cinema. The noted documentarian John Grierson dismissed his contemporary Alfred Hitchcock as 'no more than the world's best director of unimportant pictures' (in Petley 1986: 105) while Ken Loach admits 'I enjoy everything French except for the word "genre". The idea that you start a film with an idea from another film represents decadence, backwardness, inwardness' (in Pirie 2009: 12). It may be useful at this point to recall the strange scene in *Witchfinder General,* when Stearne meets the horse trader (Wilfred Brambell), whose name is Master Loach. Could this be a dig at the director of *Cathy Come Home* (1966) and *Poor Cow* (1967) whose social realist aesthetics and sweeping dismissal of all things generic represent the very opposite of a film like *Witchfinder General?*

This deep-seated disregard for the fantastic, the stylised and the generic can be seen in the frequently vitriolic reaction to home-grown horror, whether it be the output of Hammer or 'disreputable classics' such as *Peeping Tom* or *Witchfinder General.*

This 'disreputability' was enhanced by the connections the genre traditionally had to the perenially seedy softcore porn industry. Tenser's background was in strip-clubs and 'nudie' films, and through him Reeves had connections to Stanley Long and Arnold

Miller, erstwhile partners in Stag Films, whose specialties included filmed strip-shows and 'glamour' photos. Long was a cinematographer who worked on the likes of *Nudes of the World* (1961) and the evocatively-titled *Take Off Your Clothes and Live* (1963) before shooting *The Sorcerers* while Miller directed *London in the Raw* (1964) and *Primitive London* (1965) before becoming Associate Producer on a number of Tigon pictures, including both of Reeves' films. Both men would return to sexploitation in the 1970s, Long with *Groupie Girl* (1970) and *The Wife-Swappers* (1970), Miller with *Sex Farm* aka *Frustrated Wives* (1973). This sex film/horror cross-over shouldn't be seen as unique to Tigon, however: a number of important figures in British horror cut their teeth on soft-porn/sexploitation, including Robert Hartford-Davis, Pete Walker and Norman J. Warren.

Another important factor that delayed the emergence of a home-grown horror cinema was over-enthusiastic censorship. *Frankenstein* (1931) and *King Kong* (1933) were cut and Tod Browning's masterpiece *Freaks* (1932) went unreleased in the UK until 1963. There are even accounts of the BBFC considering a ban on *The Cabinet of Dr. Caligari* (1919) for fear it would upset those who had relatives in asylums (see Kermode, 1997).[2]

The Ghoul (1933), starring Boris Karloff as an undead Egyptologist, is widely regarded as the first British horror film. But it spawned few imitators, although there was a series of 'horrific' films made throughout the 1930s, which sought to avoid the censor's scissors by smuggling 'horror into comedies and thrillers rather than attempting to make outright horror films' (Conrich 1997: 228). The lurid output of Tod Slaughter, such as *Maria Marten* (1935) and *Sweeney Todd, The Demon Barber of Fleet Street* (1936), was sold as old-fashioned, barn-storming melodrama, updating a very British theatrical tradition.

Similarly, the influential anthology picture *Dead of Night* (1945) is a landmark Ealing Studios film whose influence appeared limited (until the 1960s when the production company Amicus would make a series of anthology horrors that obsessively reworked elements of the earlier film). There were a number of ghost films made in the 1940s, in no small part due to the sense of loss engendered by the Second World War.

As with AIP, the emergence of the teenage demographic in the 1950s was crucial to the emergence of the British horror film. As television replaced cinema as the family-friendly medium, the film industry discovered a new potential audience in the young. In 1951 the censor replaced the H with the X certificate, for viewers 18 and over, and Hammer, a small company formed back in the 1930s, was quick to take advantage of the new freedoms it afforded.

From a twenty-first century vantage point, with the re-released Hammer *Dracula* (1958) being certificated '12A' and Royal Mail printing a series of Hammer stamps, it's easy to lose sight of how shocking the company's output was and what critical contempt it generated. Carlos Clarens, in his celebrated study 'Horror Movies' (1971) is forthright:

> the common denominator of their product is not horror but sadism. The more jaded the public's palate becomes, the ranker the banquet of effects...Mutilations, beheadings, gougings, burning flesh, and decaying corpses – all of these are arbitrarily spliced into the scenarios at the expense of characterisation and plot. (1971: 209)

Reviewing one of the studio's first gothic horrors for 'The Daily Worker', Nina Hibbin told how she:

> went to see *Dracula*, a Hammer film, prepared to enjoy a nervous giggle. I was even ready to poke gentle fun of it (sic.) I came way revolted and outraged. (1959: 2)

Her experience anticipates that of Alan Bennett, who similarly expected laughs from *Witchfinder General*, only to be equally appalled. It seems that horror films that frighten or disturb rather than amuse, are a shock to many viewers. Perhaps the best-known and certainly the most vituperative attack on Hammer came from Derek Hill in 'Sight and Sound'. In his 1958/9 article, 'The Face of Horror', Hill spluttered:

> Only a sick society could bear the hoardings, let alone the films. Yet the displays, the posters and the slogans have become an accepted part of the West End scene. So, too, have the queues. The horror boom...is still prospering. Why? (1958/9: 6)

He goes on to claim that 'details immediately reminiscent of concentration camp atrocities are common' (1958/9: 9) in British horror films before stating:

> most of these new films [from Hammer, as well as sci-fi films such as *The Fly* and *The Trollenberg Terror*] merely attempt to outdo each other in the flat presentation of revolting details which are clearly regarded as their principal box-office assets...These sequences apart, the films have little *raison d'etre*. Nothing could be duller, for instance,

> than the 'plot' sequences which bridge the sensational sections of the [Hammer] Frankenstein films. (Ibid.)

Again, it's hard to avoid the irony, that Hill finds Hammer films 'revolting' in comparison to earlier horror films and only ten years later, an equally-incensed Bennett would find *Witchfinder General* 'a degrading experience', rather than the 'blood and guts' and 'belly laughs' of other genre pictures (perhaps those same Hammer films rendered palatable by the passing of time?). For Hammer, such critical disdain was matched by commercial success. Indeed, it may be that this oft-expressed distaste helped market their lurid, gruesome offerings to a sensation-hungry public. Certainly, Hammer executive/producer/director Michael Carreras seemed to fear the embrace of the critical establishment:

> When the National Film Theatre gave us a two-week season I was terrified. I thought if they made us respectable, it would ruin our whole image. (in Hutchings 1993: 187)

Hammer's impressive box-office returns led to the emergence of a number of companies specialising in horror including Amicus, Anglo-Amalgamated and Tony Tenser's Tigon.

However, by the mid-1960s the Hammer brand, although still popular, was starting to look formulaic. It's not that the films were bad: the Cornish-set double bill from 1966, *The Reptile* and *Plague of the Zombies* are notable works and a number of the late Hammer films are strikingly off-beat, from *Countess Dracula* (1971) and *Vampire Circus* (1972) to the 'hip' psycho-thriller *Straight on Till Morning* (1972) and *Blood from the Mummy's Tomb* (1973), written by Christopher Wicking, another Siegel fan and one-time Reeves associate. It was more that their above-mentioned ability to shock had dissipated and a kind of familiarity, even cosiness was setting in. One notable example of Hammer's reluctance to deviate from their successful formulae was the decision to turn down Polanski's *Cul-de-Sac*, deeming it 'rather macabre' (Sandford 2007: 102). It is also apparent that when Hammer did attempt to 'spice up' their product in the early 1970s, it wasn't with the kind of gore contemporary American and European genre films were doling out but with soft-core sex, exemplified by the 'tits and fangs' of the Karnstein trilogy (1970–2).

Hammer also consciously avoided the social upheaval of the 1960s. *The Devil Rides Out* (1968) is one of their best films but its indeterminate period setting is telling. By the time they made a 'Swinging London' picture, *Dracula AD 1972* (1972) with its would-be hipsters hanging out in Kings Road coffee bars, the moment had well and truly passed. Of course, this reluctance to (pardon the pun) inject new blood or to deal with contemporary Britain was not solely down to stuffiness on the part of the middle-aged 'squares' at Hammer. Generic cycles are constantly in flux and horror cinema is particularly prone to this. In the 1930s and 40s, the Universal monster series started a craze for horror and produced many of the genre's classics, such as *Frankenstein* and *The Wolf Man* (1941). However, they inevitably began to rely heavily on sequels, which in turn ended up as 'multiple monster' films, such as *Frankenstein Meets the Wolf Man* (1943) and *House of Frankenstein* (1944), which adds Dracula, a mad doctor and hunchback. Then came the inevitable lapse into outright parody with a number of 'Abbot and Costello meet the monsters' vehicles.

In the late 1970s and early 80s, the slasher cycle that flourished after the huge success of *Halloween* (1978) and *Friday the 13th* (1980) quickly became exhausted and once again, parodies emerged (*Saturday the 14th* [1981]) A more recent example would be that of *Scream* (1996), which was a semi-parody in itself, being followed only four years later by the witless *Scary Movie* (2000) and its numerous sequels.

This is the pattern that re-emerged at Hammer: all in all, they produced seven Dracula films starring Lee while Cushing played Frankenstein six times. The affectionate gothic spoofs *Carry On Screaming* (1966) and Polanski's *Dance of the Vampires* (1967) are indicative of how familiar the Hammer studio style had become.

At the same time, however, this situation threw up opportunities for the enterprising would-be auteur. As David Pirie says of British horror in the mid-sixties:

it did represent an established cinematic field in Britain, where almost for the first time the aspiring film-maker could work within a tentative cultural tradition...a tradition that by this time had lost some of its original rigidity and was beginning to hunt for new talent and new ideas. (2009: 175)

Reeves, like Polanski before him, found a comfortable generic niche, producing work that was influenced by the gothic tradition while at the same time reacting against it.

One of the striking differences between Hammer's output and *Witchfinder* is the treatment of 'evil'. Reeves and Baker's script substitutes a palpable moral horror and a scathing depiction of inhumanity for the more familiar Manichean morality and reassuring climactic restoration of order, as well as locating their brutality in a recognisable England (rather than the comfortably distanced mittel-European settings of many Hammer films).

Reeves was clear about his desire to portray 'the evil that men do', saying:

> I'm interested in the depths of human degradation. Just how far you and I can sink. (quoted in Murray 2002: 127)

Terence Fisher, the most prolific and arguably best-regarded director from the Hammer stable, described his response to *Witchfinder* in a 1974 interview.

> I liked it to a point. I didn't like it to a point...I found it, in a strange way, not satisfying but upsetting...It was effective, I'm not arguing about this and I'll admit the film craft was tremendous. But, I found it emotionally upsetting. (in Jensen 2008: 62)

Fisher's comment in the same interview offers a perfect illustration of the difference between his films and those of Reeves:

> ultimately and inevitably, Good must be triumphant – not in every particular case in our experience of life – but ultimately and inevitably it is going to be. (Ibid.)

Consequently, for Hammer, religion, with its comforting delineation between good and evil and its belief in the triumph of the former over the latter, is largely regarded as a positive force. In their *Dracula Has Risen from the Grave* (1968), made the same year as Reeves' film, we are offered the bizarre spectacle of the Count impaled on a stake but refusing to die because the atheist hero won't pray (a scene that Christopher Lee wisely objected to although he was over-ruled).

In contrast, *Witchfinder* is littered with ineffectual or corrupted prayers. It starts with a clergyman reading from his prayerbook as he presides over a hanging and ends with the words 'May God have mercy on us all' (a variation on Bassett's last line of dialogue,

'God forgive us' [1966: 250]). Elsewhere, Marshall explains to his Captain his reasons for deserting. As the Cornet leaves, the Captain mutters to himself 'May God help you in your search, Cornet Marshall', a search that will however end in insanity and chaos. All of these invocations are shown to be meaningless in this savage, godless world.

Reeves' film also belongs to a loose group of 'historical horrors' that had been explored by Hammer, amongst others. Examples of this disparate sub-genre where past events are exploited for an array of gruesome spectacles include *Tower of London* (1939), *Corridors of Blood* (1958), the Val Lewton projects *The Body Snatcher* (1945) and *Bedlam* (1946), Hammer's *Stranglers of Bombay* (1960) and *Rasputin the Mad Monk* (1965) and Ken Russell's *The Devils* (1971) and *Gothic* (1986). Whether home-grown work with a foreign setting (such as Hammer's Berkshire Bombay) or Hollywood pictures set in a backlot Olde England, these films often have a pronounced British flavour.

The success of British horror in this period can be gauged by the numbers of genre films released. In 1967, *The Sorcerers* was one of eleven home-grown horror films, three of which were made by Hammer. The following year, there were ten, including *Witchfinder*, seven of which were from Hammer. By 1971, there were an incredible twenty-five British horror films released, seven of which were from Hammer. (This boom didn't last long. By 1975, there were only five released, none of which were from Hammer.)

This production escalation explains why AIP wanted in and their involvement brought Louis 'Deke' Hayward on board, their man in London, who had a not-entirely unjustified reputation for meddling in the projects he was involved in. Hayward's writing credit ('additional scenes by') seems to gave been more contractual than anything, like Arnold Miller's producer credit. Benjamin Halligan describes Hayward's claim (repeated over the years) to have written any of the film as 'entirely fictitious' (2003: 117). He seems to have supervised one of the 'continental' scenes (what Kim Newman [2003] dubbed 'tavern roistering') shot by Tenser and spliced into the European cut.

PLEASANCE, PRICE AND EICHMANN

In an attempt to counterbalance 'Deke' Hayward's involvement, Reeves invited Phillip

Waddilove to serve as location manager. Waddilove contributed £5,000 to Tigon's half of the budget, in return for an Associate Producer credit. One of AIP's demands in particular put them at odds with the director. They wanted Vincent Prince to play Hopkins, in part to create some continuity between *Witchfinder* and their lucrative Poe series. However, Reeves and Baker had written the part with Donald Pleasance in mind. His Witchfinder would have been a very different one.

A fine character actor, Pleasance was short, ugly and unafraid to be down-trodden and pathetic: consider his put-upon *Dr. Crippen* (1962), the cross-dressing husband in Polanski's *Cul-de-Sac* or his ex-army matchseller in *From Beyond the Grave* (1973). Certainly, the snivelling, self-pitying Hopkins of the novel is more Pleasance than Price:

> Matthew Hopkins might have been any age between thirty and forty-five. An inch shorter than Stearne, (who is described as 'of middle height') he was also slighter of build and his short, square-cropped beard showed signs of premature grey. His eyes, slightly bulbous, were a watery blue and his hair and hands were well-kept. There was little about his appearance, however, to mark him out from the hundreds of others about him or to stamp him more indelibly upon the memory. (Bassett 1966: 13)

Pleasance's Hopkins would have been the archetypal 'little man', drunk on power and keen to compensate for his shortcomings by doling out pain and death, a kind of seventeenth century Adolf Eichmann. Eichmann, 'the architect of the Holocaust', captured in 1960 and put on trial in Israel, inspired journalist Hannah Arendt's famous and oft-repeated quote about the 'banality of evil'. Pleasance could easily have played such a sadistic penpusher but there is precious little banality in Price's evil. For a start, he's too tall, too handsome and too charismatic.

For Robin Wood, the star is the one jarring element in the film,

> a central flaw. Vincent Price does not really belong in it...He gives a very accomplished performance but he remains always Vincent Price in costume. *Witchfinder General*, while certainly horrific, is not really a genre horror film and it is the genre that Price's presence continually evokes. (1969: 6)

If there is, in fact, a problem with the central performance, it's Price's undeniable presence. With his noble features, courtly manner and almost-aristocratic air, he can't help but make Hopkins into an imposing character, a character who is, as Justin Smith (2006) suggests, reminiscent of Milton's Satan.

AIP got their way and this led to some bad blood between director and star. Phillip Waddilove has recalled how he met the star at the airport, only to be told 'Take me to your goddamn young genius' (in Halligan 2002: 117). Certainly, Price seems to have been in little doubt that he was not the preferred choice of this 'goddamn young genius'. Also, the actor had found a comfortable niche in the Corman films, often relying on little more than his considerable presence and his unique voice, and so it must have been irritating to be told, in no uncertain terms, what to do by the relatively inexperienced Reeves.

There has been some speculation that Price had sexual designs on Reeves but this is hard to substantiate (for obvious reasons). A number of sources suggest the actor was gay/bisexual: Harry M. Benshoff writes of his 'gay resonances' (1997:213) and his 'queer male diva persona' (2008), although for Price's biographer, Lucy Chase Williams such claims are groundless (see Williams 1995). Tony Tenser clearly thought Price's behaviour was, in part, sexually motivated, telling John Hamilton, 'I also think that Vincent had a crush on Mike and when Mike treated him so indifferently he was hurt' (2005: 108). However, some accounts suggest a much more prosaic reason for the actor's bad humour, namely that he had just quit smoking (see Murray 2002).

What is undeniable is that the horror of *Witchfinder General* is not Price's kind of horror. Even when decapitating a sleeping Arthur Lowe and sticking his head on a milk bottle or force-feeding Robert Morley his poodles in *Theatre of Blood*, Price's broad playing and comic-book relish ensures the sadism is only ever semi-serious. David Thomson considers it 'a paradox that he should be the king of that genre [horror], for he knew that no one was really frightened by that old humbug' (2002: 699). Certainly, some of the actor's public pronouncements suggest a playfullness clearly at odds with *Witchfinder's* graphic torture scenes: 'I have never been realistic but I hope that I have been stylish' (in Hutchinson 1996: 259).

Price's performance is, without a doubt, highly untypical and all the more affecting for it. For many, this is the work of the director: Reeves put a great deal of pressure on the actor to get him to 'tone it down': as Paul Ferris put it :'this thing of saying "Vincent, down, down, down". All the time it was "down'"(quoted in Murray 2002: 182).

AIP's Sam Arkoff certainly gave the credit to Reeves:

> Michael Reeves brought out some element in Vincent that hadn't been seen in a long
> time. Vincent was more savage in that picture, Michael really brought out the balls in
> him. I was surprised how terrifying Vincent was in that. I hadn't expected it...There was
> a malevolence, a malignance about Vincent in that role. (quoted in Murray 2002: 245)

But Leon Hunt argues that Price's performance 'is not restrained, it's cold – stone
cold as befits the model of masculinity he embodies in the film' (1996: 127). There is a
moment when his composure momentarily cracks and it's possibly the only time when
one can empathise with the sociopathic Hopkins: when he learns of Stearne's rape
of Sara, he turns away and closes his eyes before walking on. Price's reactive playing
makes the scene extremely effective, managing to complicate our response to the
witchfinder. The casting of Price rather than Pleasance led to Reeves having to ditch
much of the psychological background Bassett's novel gives Hopkins and remove some
of the incidents designed to underline the character's status as a 'little man' (such as the
scene where he falls off his horse, to the amusement of watching villagers). Instead, this
Hopkins is shown as a remote presence betraying very little emotion, what Halligan has
called 'an English Civil War Lee Marvin – efficient, deadly, single-minded and charismatic'
(2003: 175), no doubt referring to the latter's performance in Siegel's *The Killers* (1964),
while David Pirie refers to the character's 'superb presence of inexorable vindictiveness'
(2009: 173).

*Sociopathic,
charismatic and
tall*

Notice how often Price is shot from below, emphasising his height (6'2"). Robin Wood has written how the actor's 'accent repeatedly jars in an otherwise all-British cast' (1969: 6) but Justin Smith is more convincing when he says:

> his theatrically urbane American accent, a slow, almost caressive, certainly hypnotic delivery, and a fleeting smile, lend Hopkins a charismatic authority in excess of the narrative realism of this very English picture. (2006: 111)

There are times when Price's unique voice and excellent timing work to devastating effect. The best example of this is the scene where Lowes opens his door to be confronted by the witchfinders and his accusers. There is a short pause before Hopkins asks 'John Lowes?'

It does seem that the actor was impressed with the final film. In a letter to Reeves sent in 1968, he describes it as 'a very impressive, moving and exciting picture! Congratulations!' (in Murray 2002: 247). After going on to praise the 'contrasts of the superb scenery and the brutality', he goes on to display considerable grace when he says:

> So, my dear Michael, in spite of the fact that we didn't get along too well – mostly my fault as I was physically and mentally indisposed at that particular moment of my life (public and private) – I do think you have made a very fine picture and what's more I liked what you gave me to do. (Ibid.)

CASTING

As was typical for a British film of this period, the cast was a mixture of affordable, lesser-known talent and some familiar faces, some in the smallest of cameo roles. The role of Marshall went, unsuprisingly, to Ian Ogilvy. The actor had first worked with Reeves on his home-made shorts and had starred in both of his previous features. After *Witchfinder*, his most significant roles would be on television, including such popular shows as *Upstairs, Downstairs* and *I, Claudius*. In 1978, he starred in *The Return of the Saint*, taking over the titular role of the debonair detective Simon Templar from Roger Moore.

Hilary Dwyer had appeared in the cult TV shows *The Prisoner* and *The Avengers* when she was cast as Sara Lowes. She would go on to have a short-lived career as a 'scream queen', teaming up with Price again in genre fare such as *The Oblong Box* (1969) and *Cry of the Banshee* (1970). She stopped acting in the mid-1970s and became a talent agent and a succesful film producer (*An Awfully Big Adventure* [1995], *Nil By Mouth* [1997]), under her married name, Heath.

Nicky Henson played Marshall's fellow soldier, Swallow. A friend of the director, he was, like Ogilvy and Dwyer, only in his early twenties. Aside from the memorable cult horror film, *Psychomania* (1973), with its undead bikers, a satanic frog and Beryl Reid, he would go on to become a familiar face on television.

A number of the performers were already familiar from popular TV shows. In the role of John Lowes, Rupert Davies was a household name in the role of the titular French detective in 'Maigret' from 1960-3. He also appeared in some high-profile films, such as *The Criminal* (1960) and *The Spy Who Came in from the Cold* (1965). He was another of the *Witchfinder* cast who turned up in *The Oblong Box*, as well as being memorably pathetic in Pete Walker's *Frightmare* (1974). He died in 1976.

Robert Russell was the oafish, brutal John Stearne. He also popped-up in some of some of the best-known TV of the 60s and 70s, including *Softly, Softly*, *Department S*, *The Persuaders* and *The Sweeney*, often in small roles as cops or thugs. The year before *Witchfinder*, he played Anger in the cult comedy *Bedazzled* (1967). Russell's voice was regarded as too thin and reedy for his character and he was dubbed in post-production by Bernard Kay, who appears in the film as the fisherman. (However, Bill Kelley [1991] has cast some doubt on this oft-repeated story, arguing that Russell's voice in the following year's *Inspector Clouseau* is the same as it is in *Witchfinder*.)

Patrick Wymark appears in one scene as Cromwell and also provides the opening voice-over. Wymark worked in television for years and would have been familiar to many viewers from his role in the corporate drama *The Power Game*. He had memorable roles in the likes of *The Criminal* (alongside Rupert Davies) and *Where Eagles Dare* (1968) and did impressive work in a number of off-beat horror films such as Polanski's *Repulsion*, *The Skull* (1965) and the *Witchfinder*-inspired *Blood on Satan's Claw*. By the time the latter film was released, Wymark was dead, after suffering a heart attack on a theatrical tour of Australia, aged only 44.

The Irish actor, Wilfred Brambell, one of the stars of the popular BBC sit-com *Steptoe and Son*, has a small but notable cameo. Indeed, this briefest of appearances from a TV actor with such a distinctive voice and familiar face may have an unintentionally disorientating effect on some viewers. But *Witchfinder General* is far from unique in this respect. A great many British films feature brief appearances by actors familiar from popular TV, whether it be Roy Castle in *Dr. Terrors House of Horrors* (1964), Leonard Rossiter in Kubrick's *Barry Lyndon* (1975) or Rik Mayall's wordless appearance at the start of *American Werewolf in London* (1981). Sometimes, this displacement can only be fully appreciated with hindsight, such as Andrew Sachs' (*Fawlty Towers'* Manuel) role as a cannibal's victim in *Frightmare* (1974), George Cole and Dennis Waterman, the two future stars of *Minder*, appearing in the same scene in *Fright* (1971) and the bizarre one-off pairing of Keith Chegwin and Roman Polanski in the latter's *Macbeth* (1971).

MORRIS JAR

A large part of the film's power comes from its majestic score by Paul Ferris, who also appears in the film using the pseudonym Morris Jar (after Maurice Jarre, who composed the music for a number of acclaimed films including *Lawrence of Arabia* [1962]). The score evokes 'Greensleeves', a piece that represents Englishness and this resemblance was intentional:

> What I was aiming for was my own 'Greensleeves'. Because 'Greensleeves' for England is like 'Danny Boy' for Ireland. (quoted in Murray 2002: 203)

According to the composer, Reeves was inspired by Elmer Bernstein's score for *The Magnificent Seven* (1960), a film that the director had seen '300 times' (quoted in Muray 2002: 204). This led him to ask Ferris to come up with what he called 'English western music' (Ibid.) Indeed, The 'Love Theme from Witchfinder General' by the Roberto Mann Orchestra, released as a single in 1968, gives the song a lush, lounge-lizard treatment that reveals the Ennio Morricone influence buried in Ferris's score. The composer was so committed to the project that he used some of his fee to pay for extra time in the recording studio. This makes the subsequent removal of his score all the more poignant.

For the US home-video release, Ferris's music was replaced by a synth score by Kendall

Schmidt. This has to be seen as, at best, crass and at worst, calculated mutilation. For some, this is one of the reasons that *Witchfinder* didn't become a cult film in North America to the degree it did it Europe.

THE UN-SWINGING SIXTIES

Unlike the Hammer product of the 1960s, *Witchfinder* reflects the political upheaval of this turbulent decade. Much of the power of the film arises from the tension between genre conventions and wider, social concerns with Reeves obliquely addressing topical issues such as the war in Vietnam and the growing 'generation gap'. In this context, the subtle anachronisms in the film can be seen as part of a deliberate strategy, a way to make a film which is as much about the 1960s as it is the 1640s. In that sense, *Witchfinder General* is in a tradition of British period films that aim to capture the contemporary *zeitgeist* such as Laurence Olivier's adaptation of *Henry V* (1944) and the Gainsborough melodrama, *The Wicked Lady* (1945).

The director also seems to have been influenced to some degree by the Peter Watkins film, *Culloden* (1964). Made for BBC TV, *Culloden* uses the eighteenth-century Scottish battle to evoke the Vietnam war through the use of amateur actors and hand-held camera. As Watkins puts it, 'we made and edited our film as if it was happening in front of news cameras and deliberately reminiscent of scenes from Vietnam which were appearing on TV at that time' (2009).

The Vietnam war left a mark on a number of popular genres in the 1960s. The war film (*The Dirty Dozen* [1968]), the Western (*The Wild Bunch* [1968]), the gangster film (*Bonnie and Clyde* [1967]) and the horror film (*Night of the Living Dead* [1968]). While the only Hollywood offering to tackle the conflict in South-East Asia directly, John Wayne's *The Green Berets* (1968) was widely derided, images from and echoes of the war turned up in a number of films (could anybody watching the long-haired, dope smoking proto-hippies in Robert Altman's Korean War comedy *MASH* [1970] miss the many Vietnam references?).

The film's relatively modest budget put paid to the sweeping battle scenes found in the book. The script featured the Battle of Naseby but in the finished film, we only see the preparations for the battle and a victorious Cromwell. The opening sniper attack on Marshall's platoon is particularly evocative of Vietnam. Snipers hiding in the undergrowth are strongly associated with the war in the public consciousness, as much as stoned G.I.s, burning villages and napalm. Like the stereotypical Viet-Cong, the attacking King's men are barely seen, hidden away like a murderous Other.

Viet-Cong-style snipers transposed to East Anglia

Of course, the much-vaunted 'Summer of Love' amounted to far more than the stereotypical images of long-hairs in tie-dyed shirts smoking pot. There were student protests and demonstrations in cities including Paris, Chicago and West Berlin. An anti-war demonstration in London's Grosvenor Square in March 1968 (in which Reeves participated) turned violent, resulting in a lot of smashed windows and over 200 arrests.

In popular culture, The Beatles may have sang 'All You Need is Love' but there was also a whiff of brimstone in the air: among the many faces on the cover of their 'Sergeant Pepper's Lonely Hearts Club Band' (1967) album, was 'the wickedest man in the world', Aleister Crowley; while The Rolling Stones revelled in Satanic imagery, with their 'Sympathy for the Devil' and friendship with the film-maker and occultist Kenneth Anger.

In the cinema, a number of British films rejected the Carnaby Street, mini-skirts and Mini-Cooper clichés, including Roman Polanski's clinically creepy *Repulsion* and Robert Hartford-Davis's sleazy *Corruption* (1967). Reeves' nihilistic genre films can therefore be seen, paradoxically, as of the times while also reacting against them (in much the same way as they are in a British gothic horror tradition while also distanced from, even critical of, that tradition). For Peter Hutchings, Reeves was the:

first to articulate a youthful viewpoint in British horror, challenging in an aggressive and systematic way the paternalism of the tradition...Reeves' films remain the most intense and disturbing expressions of this moment of change. (1993: 270)

There is a curious symmetry to many of the events of this strange, noisy and much-dissected decade . By 1969, the year Reeves died, Beatles fan Charles Manson would have ordered the killing of, amongst others, Polanski's wife, Sharon Tate while The Rolling Stones concert at Altamont that same year would end in a knife murder caught on camera. The organisation English Heretic, whose stated aim is to 'maintain, nurture and care for the psychohistorical environment of England', have posited the (semi-serious?) suggestion that *Witchfinder's* witch-burning in the Suffolk village of Lavenham may just be the catalyst for all this dystopian bloodletting. In their article, 'The Curse of the Conqueror Worm', they claim to have uncovered

a sinister connection between Lavenham and the film industry. In 1969, Sharon Tate, the wife of Roman Polanski, had a role in the film, *The 13 Chairs*, a comedy horror, interior and exterior scenes of which were shot at Lavenham. In 1970, John Lennon and Yoko Ono filmed their experimental movie *Apotheosis* above the snow covered fields of Lavenham and in 1971, Pier Paolo Pasolini directed the *Canterbury Tales*, which used the Suffolk village as the location of medieval London. (English Heretic, undated)

They go on to detail the violent deaths of Tate, Pasolini (beaten to death under mysterious circumstances in 1975) and Lennon (assassinated in 1980). They posit that Reeves, aware of the curse that his witch-burning had unleashed, committed suicide just before the start of the ancient Roman festival of Parentalia, the purpose of which was to honour the dead. Although this story may seem fanciful, it's a good example of how some cult films attract rumour and speculation, the wilder the better. Mikita Brottman refers to such texts as 'cursed films', a phrase coined by the aforementioned Kenneth Anger to describe 'films involving one or more celebrities who took their own lives, all of which have come to attain an odd a kind of cult status of their own' (Brottman 2008).

The fact that Reeves' death seems to have been a tragic accident (and a reminder that downers and alcohol don't mix) shouldn't be allowed to get in the way of a good story. It's also surprising that they don't mention the early deaths of a number of the

Witchfinder cast and crew, such as Patrick Wymark, cinematographer Coquillon and composer/actor Ferris.

In *The Sorcerers*, Reeves offers many of the superficial signifiers of the 'sixties scene' – mini-skirted dollybirds, night-clubs, pop music – but places them in a milieu which is more seedy than groovy. Ian Sinclair has evocatively described the world of the film:

> Its horizons are pinched and mean...*Sorcerers* (sic.) remains resolutely stopped down, locked in the skull, an unacknowledged and genuine contribution to London's covert filmography. (1997: 291)

In much the same way as *The Sorcerers* features a search for mind-expanding kicks that ends in multiple murder, so *Witchfinder's General's* association of sexuality with rape, brutality, coercion and torture can be read as a sour comment on the sexually-liberated 'permissive society'.

17th century free love

Certainly, the lyrical, dissolve-heavy sex scene would seem to be more 1960s than 1640s (as is Ogilvy's hair-style: Robin Wood [1969] has noted how the actor wears the same floppy hair playing both Mike Roscoe and Richard Marshall).

In the book, the coupling of Margery and Sara is heavily implied, although Sara later tells Hopkins she is a virgin. The contemporary sexual mores of the film were not lost on the BBFC examiner who read the script:

> the only relief from the violence is found in sex and nudity which seems rather out of place in a story about Puritans and an innocent girl in the 17th century. (in Halligan 2003: 121)

The dissolve from lovemaking to Hopkins and Stearne is a perfect illustration of the film's gloomy worldview, with cruelty and chaos never far away. This abrupt shift from 'love-in' to despair and violence also, presciently, seems to anticipate the crashing comedown that was to follow the loved-up, fuzzy vision of the 60s enshrined in popular mythology.

THE SHOOT

The production shot from mid-September to mid-November 1967. The importance of landscape to the film meant that it wasn't an option to do as Hammer often did and shoot on backlots in Berkshire. The Suffolk locations included the stately home, Kentwell Hall (where the accused witches are swum), the Market Square in the aforementioned village of Lavenham (for the witch-burning), the coastal town of Dunwich (the scene with the fisherman) and Orford Castle (the climactic scene).

Locations in Norfolk included the church in Rusford (which doubled as John Lowes' church) while the horse-riding sequences were shot on the army training site known as the Stanford Battle Area. The scene where Stearne makes his escape on horseback was shot in Langley Country Park, Slough while the attempted ambush of Marshall's patrol was shot in Black Park. This Buckinghamshire country park is frequently used as a filming location, largely due to its proximity to Pinewood Studios: a number of Hammer and Carry On films, a couple of Bond adventures and the recent *Eden Lake* (2008) all had sequences shot in and around there.

The aforementioned tension between the director and his star worsened thoughout the shoot. At one point, Reeves told Price to shoot a pistol while mounted on his horse. Although the actor objected, the director was insistent, so Price fired and, predictably, was thrown to the floor. A number of accounts suggest Reeves was particularly annoyed by Price's habit of eating the wine gums stowed away in his boots during takes. During the final scene, Price arrived a bit the worse for wear, having started drinking earlier in the evening and Reeves responded furiously, telling Ogilvy to 'hit him as hard as you can' (in Murray 2002: 241).

As the shoot drew to a close, it became clear there was still a major problem with the film: it didn't have an ending. The script had Stearne clash with a band of gypsies, raping one of their women and ending up being blinded and then impaled. Marshall then enlisted their help in capturing Hopkins and, as in Bassett's novel, the Witchfinder would be 'swum' and hanged. But Tenser, ever the producer, balked at having to hire more extras to play the gypsies, so Reeves and cast had to improvise an ending (examined further in Chapter 3).

For a low-budget period film made on location, the shoot was surprisingly smooth. The reaction to the finished film would be anything but.

THE CENSORS

The problems with the censors had begun at the script stage. According to Benjamin Halligan, the first draft included beheadings, eye-gouging, a staking and a scene where a shot soldier flew through the air before colliding with a tree. The script was returned to Tenser with a letter which began:

> We have now read your script Witchfinder General and are greatly disturbed by it. It could fairly be described as a study in sadism in which every detail of suffering and cruelty is lovingly dwelt on. (in Halligan 2003: 121)

It goes onto to complain that:

> There are few pages on which some helpless human being is not shown being hanged, burned, drowned, raped, beaten-up, dragged-about or otherwise bullied and threatened. (Ibid.)

The Director of the BBFC at that time was John Trevelyan, reportedly a distant cousin of Reeves. Trevelyan was and remains a polarising, often contradictory figure, whose tenure at the BBFC (from 1958-1971) coincided with a great many changes in film culture: the rise of European art cinema with its explorations of 'adult' themes, the emergence of the counter-culture and the accompanying changes in attitudes to issues such as sex and drugs and the 'golden age' of the British horror film.

In his memoir 'What The Censor Saw' (1973), Trevelyan is at pains to paint himself as an enlightened, liberal fellow:

There are, and will continue to be, some films that might be harmful to some people, but I believe that this risk is not great enough to justify the continuance of restricting the freedom of adults. (1973: 229)

Elsewhere, he writes of his friendships with directors such as Stanley Kubrick, John Schlesinger and Joseph Losey and his meetings with Bergman and Hitchcock. However, for all his much-vaunted liberalism, he had no qualms in making cuts to *The Silence* (1963) and even the shower murder in *Psycho* (1960) 'to lessen the sadism' (1973: 160). Trevelyan was even shameless enough to cut some of the death camp footage in the Alain Resnais Holocaust documentary, *Nuit et Brouillard* (1955), to remove 'the worst of the horrors' (1973: 173)!

There is no doubt, though, that he was liked by a number of film-makers. Interviewed for the BBC documentary *Empire of the Censors* (1995), both Polanski and Donald Cammell speak fondly of him.

But Trevelyan, like many critics, seems to have regarded horror films with particular distaste. Consider his thoughts on Mario Bava's landmark *La maschera del demonio* aka *Black Sunday*:

A film called *Black Sunday* was refused a certificate in 1961 on grounds of disgust, but was eventually passed by the Board in 1968 because by that time it looked rather ridiculous... One help to us was that nobody took these films seriously; this included the people who made them as well as the audiences (1973: 166).

Mark Kermode offers a neat riposte to Trevelyan's idiotic comments, suggesting that, on the contrary:

no one was allowed to take these films seriously, for only when they had passed into the realm of ridicule were they finally considered acceptable for public viewing. (2002: 14)

On the subject of screen violence, again, Trevelyan comes across as the voice of reason, declaring how he had:

always believed that violence in a film, even if explicit and horrifying, was justified if it was there for a valid purpose, particularly to show that violence was inhuman and totally destructive. (1973: 162)

After discussing the two films he felt exemplified this approach (*Soldier Blue* [1970] and *The Devils* [1971]), he turns to *Witchfinder*:

> This film gave the impression that it was exploiting violence and in particular sadism, for commercial reasons, but knowing the director well, I knew that this was not his intention; he detested violence and, as he told me at the time, set out to show how horrible and degrading it was, but to us at the Board his sincere intention did not come though on the screen and we felt obliged to make extensive cuts before passing it. (Ibid.)

Trevelyan goes on to explain how Reeves withdrew from the cutting of his film but later seemed to recant, writing to say that 'the cuts had been very well made and had not harmed the film nearly as much as he had expected' (1973: 163).

This may not be entirely true. When Trevelyan saw a rough cut of the film in early 1968, he seemed to have had no problems with it: 'I do not think this films (sic.) is likely to give us much trouble' (quoted in Halligan 2003: 152). But after seeing the finished film, he changed his mind and ordered cuts to a number of scenes, including the torture of Lowes, the witch-burning and Marshall's climactic axe attack on Hopkins.

Before the cuts had been made, Reeves wrote an impassioned letter to Trevelyan, attempting to justify the violence in his film (the full transcript of this letter can be found in both Murray [2002] and Halligan [2003]). Particularly interesting are the director's comments about the morality of the film, which, he argued:

> lies in its whole content; and the fact that in the final 90 seconds the violence explodes utterly in the face of the 'sympathetic' protagonists (by their own particpation in it) is the core of all that is good (morally good) in the film. (quoted in Murray 2002: 255)

Both Ian Ogilvy and Tom Baker have expressed some scepticism about these lofty claims, the fomer suggesting that the director concocted this notion of a moral purpose as a way of justifying the film's violence and then started to believe it himself (see Murray 2003). Certainly the question of Reeves' relationship to violence is a complicated one (examined further in Chapter 3).

Trevelyan does seem to have been conflicted when it came to *Witchfinder General*. He expressed what seems to be heartfelt sympathy for the director, while also acknowledging the film's considerable power. At the conclusion of his letter to the director, he admits to:

> ...regret that I under-estimated the impact of this film when I saw an assembly or rough cut. I now know the film well, and I believe that I am justified in saying that the impact was immensely heightened by colour, sound effects and music. The picture in its final form was very much stronger than I had anticipated, and it will have the effect of making me more cautious in future in making preliminary judgements on films of violence. (quoted in Murray 2002: 258)

Recent DVD releases have seen this excised footage restored. These shots are easily identifiable, with degraded colours and a fuzzy blur to the images. Looking at these scenes, it's clear that Trevelyan's problems were not about the content per se and more about a perceived gratuitous quality. So Lowes being 'pricked' once was OK but a further two shots were not. There also seems to have been an issue with the amount of blood spilled. These concerns led to cuts in a number of the most violent scenes, with the following footage removed:

- During the interrogation of the Brandeston accused, a number of shots of Stearne slapping and strangling a bloodied woman.

- Lowes, again bloodied, being tied up before being 'swum'.

- A bound witch stuggling in the water as she is 'swum'.

- Elizabeth Clarke being dragged to the ladder and lashed to it, her face bloody.

- Shots of her being lowered into the fire. Two long shots, one of her body catching fire and another of it burning.

- Sara being 'pricked'. A shot of her screaming in pain. A long shot showing Stearne 'pricking' her.

- Two shots of Hopkins being hit with the axe.

While it is refreshing to see a more complete version of *Witchfinder General* than the one initially released, any talk of a 'complete version' is problematic. For example, the 2003 Prism DVD would seem to emphasise the inclusion of the Tenser-shot extra nude scenes more than the Trevelyan-excised violence. A short text appears before the film, explaining how 'some alternate versions of certain scenes were created to cater for the more lenient foreign markets'. It goes on to say that 'this is the full export version, which includes more explicit scenes'. These scenes were not sanctioned by Reeves and would seem to have been, at best, tolerated. They certainly appear out of place, choppily edited and with mismatched lighting. There also seems to have been no effort made to have these half-naked wenches (apparently performers from London strip-clubs) actually try to act. They just pose awkwardly, with their bodices undone, while Russell's Stearne carouses, pouring beer over their heads and guffawing.

THE CRITICS

When assessing the critical reaction to *Witchfinder General*, it is instructive to consider the prevailing attitudes to horror cinema at that time, the aforementioned attacks on Hammer and the violent condemnation of *Psycho* and *Peeping Tom*. In the latter case, a typical reaction came from The Daily Express, which suggested director Powell:

> should be ashamed of himself. The acting is good. The photography is fine. But what is the result? Sadism, sex and the exploitation of human degradation. (in Rigby 2000: 86)

So extreme was the critical reaction that it was widely considered to have permanently hobbled Michael Powell's career.

The newspaper reviews of *Witchfinder* were savage. Dilys Powell in The Sunday Times called it 'peculiarly nauseating', Margaret Hinxman in The Daily Telegraph found it 'an exercise in sadistic extravagance' while in The Guardian, David Wilson opined that 'the film is less concerned with narrative than with exploiting every opportunity for gratuitous sadism' (in Murray 2002: 262-3).

Sight & Sound offered a pithy, no-star review which is worth quoting in full:

> Vincent Price as a self-appointed witch-hunter in Cromwell's England. Excessively and gratuitously sadistic, with lashings of blood and the camera lingering with relish over

rape, hangings and assorted mutilations. Fine if you like that kind of thing. (1968: 162)

The reviews were not all negative. Tom Milne of The Monthly Film Bulletin praised the 'subtle use of colour, in which the delicate patchwork greens of the English countryside... are shot through by the colours of death and decay'. Milne also noted the 'vivid sense of a time out of joint' (1968: 100) while comparing the critical reaction to that of *Peeping Tom*, noting that it is 'difficult to see why' there was such outrage: 'there are in effect only two scenes of lingering violence: the opening...and the end...In between these two extremes, the effect is oddly muted' (Ibid.).

Writing for *Films and Filming*, David Austen considered it 'a very frightening film... *Witchfinder General* is emphatically not a horror film; it is, however, a very horrifying one' (1968: 36). Austen notes the film's kinship with the Western before praising the star: 'Matthew Hopkins is the best of Price's recent performances' (Ibid.).

The most notorious attack on the film came from the playwright and performer Alan Bennett, who was the film reviewer at The Listener magazine. He began his review by compiling a list of the violent events depicted, 'I slow drowning, I double hanging, I burning at the stake in which the victim was lowered slowly on to the pyre' right through to 'a man hacked to death with an axe'. He did acknowledge that:

> Of course, blood and guts is the stuff of horror film, though, as with Victorian melodrama, what makes them popular and even healthy are the belly laughs which usually punctuate them. For these one can generally rely on the film's star, Vincent Price. But not here. There are no laughs in *Witchfinder General*. It is the most persistently sadistic and morally rotten film I have seen. It was a degrading experience, by which I mean it made me feel dirty. I would not have wasted space on such a shambles had not the film received serious and favourable critical attention in certain quarters. (in Murray 2002: 263)

After singling out John Russell Taylor of The Times (who 'emphasised its subtlety, imagination and camera-work over three columns') and Tom Milne of The Observer (who praised its 'intelligence and talent, real style and presence'), Bennett really lets rip:

> This seems to me to be pernicious rubbish. The world of film is not an autochthonous world: sadism which corrupts and repels in life continues to do so when placed on

celluloid. It is not compounded by style nor excused by camera-work. Hitler had a film made of the death throes of the plotters of July 1944. I wonder what Messrs Taylor and Milne would make of that. Purely, of course, in terms of film. (Ibid.)

As one would expect, Bennett writes with flair and wit but his criticisms echo those of Derek Hill from a decade earlier. Bennett also seems to have expected laughs but found only sadism and degradation. He seems to see no merit or skill in the film-making ('a shambles') and has no compunction in invoking Nazi atrocities. The violence of Bennett's attack incensed Reeves and he fired an angry response which was printed in the next issue. The director described Bennett's piece as a 'vitriolic condemnation of my film... and of two of the critics who were kind enough to praise it' (in Murray 2002: 264). After pointing out Bennett's assertion that the film 'made him feel dirty' and admitting that he has 'no desire to quarrel with him over the film's merits or demerits as art (whatever that may mean)', he suggests that 'Mr. Bennett and I are at least in agreement over one thing – that violence as such is more horrible than can be adequately described on paper' (Ibid.). After quoting Bennett's thoughts on the healing balm of the belly laugh in horror, Reeves starts to warm to this theme:

Surely the most immoral thing in any form of entertainment is the conditioning of the audience to accept and enjoy violence? Is this not exactly the attitude that could lead to more and more casual indulgence in violence, starting with individuals and thence spiralling nauseatingly upwards to a crescendo of international bloodletting?...Violence is horrible, degrading and sordid. Insofar as one is going to show it on the screen at all, it should be presented as such – and the more people it shocks into sickened recognition of these facts the better. I wish I could have witnessed Mr. Bennett frantically attempting to wash away the 'dirty' feeling my film gave him. It would have been proof of the fact that *Witchfinder* works as intended. (Ibid.)

The impassioned language, the painful sincerity and the hyperbole ('a crescendo of international bloodletting'?) testify to the director's sense of outrage and also, perhaps, to his youth. Certainly, Ian Ogilvy, when interviewed in 2002 for John Murray's Reeves biography, felt it was 'the writing of a very young man. It's unsophisticated' (2002: 264). It's undeniable, however, that the graphic violence of the film, coupled with considerable seriousness of intent, offers an experience far from that of the generic horror film.

It also raises serious questions about depicting violence and why we like to watch it, questions considered further in Chapter 3.

THE CONQUEROR WORM

For the US release, AIP re-titled the film *The Conqueror Worm*, after the Poe poem. A fine title for a horror film but one with no obvious connection to Reeves' film. Price was brought in to read lines from the poem and these were added to the opening and closing of the film. (Even Roger Corman fell victim to AIP's obsession with re-branding films as Poe adaptations. His 1963 adaptation of H.P. Lovecraft's 'The Case of Charles Dexter Ward' was given the Poe-derived title, *The Haunted Palace*.)

AIP's Sam Arkoff did give another (revealing) reason for the retitling, saying of Bassett's book:

> That was a bestselling book in the UK but who the hell in America cared about that, or knew about Cromwell and the rest of it. I came up with the new title. We found a way to please both worlds. (in Kelley 1991: 42)

These changes were trivial in the scheme of things: Reeves himself said 'Oh what the hell. It's still our movie, they haven't changed that' (quoted in Murray 2002: 271). Certainly a title change pales next to the other indignities heaped on the film, such as Trevelyan's cuts, the addition of the topless tavern wenches and the removal of the original score for US home video release.

As in Britain, American reviewers were divided about the film, although the good reviews took it less seriously than their British counterparts. For Variety, the whole thing was underwhelming. They regarded the final scene as 'the only really good action scene', Ogilvy as 'somewhat dashing' despite his 'one-note hero's role to play' and Reeves' scripting and direction 'mediocre' (1968). Renata Adler of The New York Times seemed to have more fun. Her review concentrates mainly on the youthful cast and (more predictably) the violence, suggesting that the:

> attractive young aspiring stars...seem to have been cast...mainly for their ability to scream. Scream as though they were being slowly burned to death, or kicked, or

poked, or stabbed – mainly about the eyes – with sticks, or shot through, or tortured, which, in fact, they are. (Adler 1968)

She notes that while some of the audience in the New Amsterdam cinema slept or quarelled through the *longeurs*, people woke up and cheered as Hopkins, 'a materialistic witch-hunter and woman disfigurer and dismemberer' (Ibid.) was hacked to death. But The Hollywood Citizen News was incensed, calling it:

a disgrace to the producers and scriptors, and a sad commentary on the art of film-making: a film with such bestial brutality and orgiastic sadism, one wonders how it ever passed customs to be released in this country. (quoted in Newman 2003)

The film was promoted in the UK with images of a be-hatted and bearded Price surrounded by a burning witch, an enticing Sara and what appears to be more extras than there are in the film. The tag-lines ranged from the underwhelming ('They reveled [sic.] in torture and murder, all in the name of justice') to the lurid ('The Year's Most Violent Film'). The US publicity campaign was more imaginative. *The Conqueror Worm* poster showed a rotting head in lurid sickly green, with burning witches and Price wrestling with a nubile woman. As well as featuring a verse of the Poe poem which spawned the title, there is the eye-grabbing tag-line: 'Leave the children at home. And if you're at all squeamish, stay at home with them.' Skilled in the art of exploitation, AIP also took out newspaper ads. These included an image of Elizabeth Clarke on fire with the caption 'burn, baby, burn' (!) and an article titled 'Sorcery Flourishing Business in Old England'. This brief 'infomercial' about the real Hopkins included the weird claim that Hopkins victims included 'few genuine witches' and a reassurance that 'he could not do it today'. Phew.

FOOTNOTES

[2] Britain failed to develop an avant-garde film culture in the 1920s and '30s for much the same reason. The BBFC refused a certificate to the first surrealist film Germaine Dulac's *The Seashell and The Clergyman* (1928), describing it as 'apparently meaningless' before adding 'if there is a meaning it is doubtless objectionable' (Robertson 1993: 39).

CHAPTER 3. ANALYSIS

I) LANDSCAPE, THE ENGLISH WESTERN AND MENTAL POLAROIDS

Landscape and history are two of the key elements of *Witchfinder General* and they are used in such a way as to consciously evoke the Western genre. With the possible exception of film noir, there is no other genre that presents the landscape as a character, rather than simply a setting. Reeves intentionally set out to produce a home-grown variant of the B-movie Westerns of Budd Boetticher and Anthony Mann. The spare, stripped-down narrative is reminiscent of Boetticher films such as *Comanche Station* (1960) while the Mann influence is even stronger. Trooper Marshall gradually comes to resemble one of the neurotic heroes played by James Stewart in the likes of *Winchester 73* (1950) and *The Naked Spur* (1953). Robin Wood describes the typical Mann protagonist as:

> neurotic, obsessive, driven, usually motivated by a desire for revenge that reduces him emotionally and morally to a brutalised condition scarcely superior to that of the villain. Hero and villain, indeed, become mirror reflections of one another. (undated)

The above is also an accurate description of Marshall and the 'doubling' that occurs with Hopkins. Wood also describes the violence in Mann's work in terms that could apply equally to *Witchfinder*, saying it is:

> never glorified: it is invariably represented as ugly, disturbing, and painful (emotionally as much as physically), and this is true as much when it is inflicted by the heroes as by the villains. (Ibid.)

However, the vengeful Western hero is almost always capable of reining his baser instincts, as Kim Newman points out:

> the Mann-Boetticher films tended to pull back at the last, before the heroes were consumed by their vengeful impulses. (2003)

Even that most ambivalent of Western protagonists, John Wayne's Ethan Edwards in *The Searchers* (1956) relents when it comes to killing his niece, whereas Marshall sacrifices everything to his bloodlust.

Many commentators have remarked upon this generic kinship, starting with Reeves himself. Interviewed in 1999, Ian Ogilvy recalled:

> I think he said do you realise we're making a Western...we're making the old galloping-across-the-countryside-in-search-of-the-bad-guy-revenge-Western.

For Kim Newman it's 'one of the few English Westerns' (1999), a very select, justifiably-unsung group made up of European co-productions like *Captain Apache* (1971) and parodies such as *Carry on Cowboy* (1966) and *A Fistful of Fingers* (1995).

But this generic influence didn't solely come from the director. Bassett's source novel also evokes the Western: both in terms of action (with characters pursuing each other on horseback through a series of small towns and villages) and thematically (the desire for revenge that drives Margery and in the latter part of the book, Hopkins). The final confrontation in the inn at Ely is reminiscent of that familiar Western trope, the showdown in the saloon. Unlike the gothic excess of the film's ending, the novel has a perfunctory climax, with Hopkins effectively subjected to 'frontier justice' and lynched.

One of the reasons for this striking use of landscape is the way Reeves and Tom Baker wrote the script around the locations. Rather than hand the completed script to a location manager, they sought out suitable scenery as they wrote. Iain Sinclair has written of how the two men:

> on a whim, took a late train out from Liverpoool Street into Suffolk. Reeves looked across the flat lands and said 'This is what it's been about all along.' They roamed East Anglia in a hired car, stopping to examine odd buildings that took their fancy, constructing a pack of mental polaroids. The narrative grew out of their discoveries. (1997: 294)

In 1999, Baker confirmed this is an interview with Andy Starke and Pete Tombs: 'What struck us was the possibility of making a film partly to do with English landscape and partly to do with movement through the geography of England and through the landscape'.

Baker's contribution to *Witchfinder General* has often been overlooked. This is, to some degree, the inevitable fate that befalls writers who co-write with directors: consider such talented yet (comparatively) little-known screenwriters as Gerard Brach (who wrote nine films with Roman Polanski), I.A.L Diamond (12 films with Billy Wilder) and Mardik Martin (who co-wrote the Scorsese films *Mean Streets* [1973] and *Raging Bull* [1980]). It's also likely that the *Witchfinder* co-writer is on occasion mistaken for his namesake, who found fame as the eponymous Timelord in *Dr. Who*. Iain Sinclair went some way to redressing the balance in his 1997 article 'Cinema Purgatorio'. Sinclair had studied with Baker in Dublin and knew him well enough to declare that *Witchfinder's* 'success lies in the tension between Baker's utopian permissiveness, his feel for the countryside and Reeves' demonic fatalism' (1997: 293).

This emphasis on landscape and movement again suggests the films of Anthony Mann: for Robin Wood, one of the distinguishing features of Mann's work is the way that 'the function of landscape is primarily dramatic...The preferred narrative structure of the films is the journey' (undated).

If *Witchfinder General* looks back to Boetticher and Mann, it also anticipates the violent revenge Westerns of the 1970s and the sexual violence in a number of them, including *Soldier Blue* (1970), *The Hunting Party* (1971) and *Chato's Land* (1972). It also predates Sam Peckinpah's notorious 'English Western', *Straw Dogs* (1971), a film which resembles *Witchfinder* both thematically and stylistically, a resemblance explored later in this chapter.

ANALYSIS: THE OPENING

A sunshine cross in a godless world

The first image of the film is the sun through leafy tree branches. The sunlight forms a cross and it's tempting to see this as the first example of the film's ironic use of religious imagery. This cross of light will be replaced by the end of the film with the red-hot metal cross Hopkins threatens to brand Sara with. This first image, of the English countryside, introduces the importance of landscape in *Witchfinder General*, a landscape which is at once familiar and alien, a beautiful backdrop to inhumanity. The camera pans down to reveal rolling green hills. There is a shot of grazing sheep, the sound of bleating, bird-song and a repeated knocking.

The presence of death in this rural idyll

In the next shot, we see the source of the sound: a man hammering at a gallows on a hill, silhouetted against a cloudy blue sky. The combination of shots suggests that the gallows is as much a part of this corner of rural England as the trees, sheep and sun. Is there a disturbing contrast going on here, between rural idyll and cruelty? Or are we supposed to see violence as just another part of the environment, as natural to this part of the world as the trees and the bird-song?

This is only the first of many times in the film that images of cruelty and death are found in the natural world. Think of the stark image of Hopkins on horseback, trotting along a road lined with poplar trees as dusk falls; the zoom out from leafy boughs to the mob leading the accused witches of Brandeston; or the dissolve from crashing waves to the fire that will consume Elizabeth Clarke.

There is a cut to a group of men dragging a bound and wailing woman past a row of cottages. The hand-held camera gets in close, the cluttered *mise-en-scène* contrasting with the earlier open spaces and spare compositions. The woman screams and a clergyman reads from the Bible in a flat, declamatory voice.

The juxtaposition of nature and brutality

As the crowd drags the woman up the hill, the camera tracks back to reveal her destination is the gallows. The sound of the wind is loud. The woman collapses in a dead faint and one of the men calls for a bucket of water. The cleric doesn't stop his emotionless incantation, the drone of his voice as much a part of this scene as the wind. The woman is soaked with the water and she awakes, dazed. She is dragged to the gallows and a shot of the eerily-still crowd reveals their blank faces. As three men lift her and put the noose around her neck, there is a striking composition, the huddle of bodies and the woman's screaming face against a great expanse of cloudy sky.

The clergyman finishes reading and nods to the executioner, who kicks the footstool away. Her scream abruptly cuts off to be replaced by the sound of the creaking gallows, as both the rolling stool and her corpse move towards the camera. One can't help but connect the trees at the start of the scene with the creaking gallows wood.

The blue sky is now cloudless. The camera slowly pans across the crowd as it begins to disperse, only seconds after the hanging. The pan stops behind the dangling woman. The sound of a martial-style drum-roll. There is a dissolve to a meadow and a startling zoom to a figure on a white horse: this may be a reference to the Biblical personification of Death, who rides 'a pale horse'. The image is transformed into a lithograph and the credit appears: 'Matthew Hopkins' followed by 'Witchfinder General'.

Matthew Hopkins

WITCHFINDER
GENERAL
© TIGON BRITISH MCMLXVIII

*The title card:
death on a pale
horse*

This opening sequence reveals much about the world of the film and introduces a number of the key themes. It's an extraordinary evocation of place and suggests a beautiful, cruel world where trees and gallows are placed alongside each other and where screams and creaking gallows are as much a part of the environment as wind and birdsong. There is misogyny, religion, violence, nature and a populace blank to the point of malevolence.

For Pirie and Wood, nature is portrayed as a positive force in the film but I think it's much less clear-cut. Halligan accurately sums up the world of the film when he talks of 'an utterly outlandish rural England' (2003: 110) and identifies 'the juxtaposition of nature and violence and the suggestion that the two are interconnected' (2003: 167). In the shooting script, there was a telling image which sadly went unfilmed, with soldiers riding past unremarked-upon corpses rotting in a ditch. Death and decay are everywhere.

Hopkins comes over as almost elemental, a baleful voyeur who is at one with this world of cruelty and blank-faced yokels, war and fire. It is Marshall who seems out of place. When the Cornet is left guarding the horses after the sniper attack on his platoon, it's as if nature itself terrifies him. He jumps and starts at every rustle and breeze. It is significant that the sounds of nature are again prominent here, the birdsong, the wind through the trees, the sound of the buzzing flies that hover around a corpse.

For a film dismissed by many as sadistic, it's interesting how often the emphasis is on nature as much, if not more, than it is on pain. After Stearne has been shot, he sits against a tree and draws his knife to remove the bullet. As he does so, the camera pans away, past birch trees and verdant woodland. We hear the sound of Stearne screaming. There is a dissolve to the sunlight through the trees, indicating the passing of time. Then a dissolve to another pan through the trees to Stearne, bloodied and unconscious. The natural world as depicted in the film is beautiful but it can be regarded as being as corrupted and warped as the people in it.

At best, the rural backdrop of *Witchfinder General* is a striking blank, as indifferent as the faces of the good folk of Lavenham, as they watch a woman being burned to death. At worst, it's a malignant world, distorted and nightmarish, governed by dark forces (a theme explored below).

II) THE CULT OF SIEGEL

The influence of Don Siegel, especially, can scarcely be over-estimated. (Pirie 2009: 168)

The American producer/director Don Siegel (1912-1991) worked in a variety of action genres: the prison film (*Riot in Cell Block 11* [1954]), the sci-fi film (*Invasion of the Body Snatchers* [1956]), war film (*Hell is for Heroes* [1962]), Western (*The Shootist* [1970]), heist movie (*Charley Varrick* [1973]) and cop thriller (*Dirty Harry* [1971]). He specialised in fast-paced stripped-down narratives, complex anti-heroic protagonists and tightly-edited action sequences. Like his fellow action auteur, Sam Fuller, Siegel managed to make art of out of formulaic genre projects in the factory context of Hollywood.

As David Thomson puts it:

He made few films that are not personal, inventive and interesting. Some are exceptional works that transcend limitations of budget, time and script... If anything, his films become more terse, more drily amused and more economically exciting. (2002: 808)

For many, Siegel is perhaps best-known for the five films he made with Clint Eastwood – from *Coogans Bluff* (1968) to *Escape From Alcatraz* (1978) – and the enormous debt Eastwood owes to his mentor has been frequently acknowledged: he cast Siegel as a laconic bar-tender in his directorial debut *Play Misty For Me* (1971) wrote the foreword to his autobiograhy and dedicated his *Unforgiven* (1992) 'To Sergio [Leone] and Don'. One indication of just how strongly Siegel was associated with 'tough guy' movies is the fact that, in addition to Eastwood, his films gave starring roles to such macho icons as Steve McQueen, John Wayne, Charles Bronson, Richard Widmark and Lee Marvin.

Siegel is interesting not only as an accomplished director of highly-personal genre films but also in his role as mentor to Reeves and Sam Peckinpah. Both men served apprenticeships as dialogue directors for Siegel and there are shared thematic and stylistic concerns in the work of all three filmmakers. Its certainly easy to see how Siegel's fast-paced, highly cinematic films appealed to Reeves, who felt little affinity with the dominant British tradition of social realism. They also had a wry, sardonic tone and a very ambiguous authorial point of view.

In addition, it's surely significant that Reeves admired Siegel, who worked exclusively in popular genres, rather than European directors like Ingmar Bergman and iconoclastic Americans like Orson Welles and John Cassavetes. Siegel would go wherever the work was, working in television when he had to (directing TV movies and episodes of *The Twilight Zone*) and taking on some very unpromising subjects (the Elvis film *Flaming Star* [1960] and *Hound-Dog Man* [1959], a vehicle for the bargain basement teen-idol Fabian). Reeves no doubt found parallels in the American's career as he himself struggled to make personal films in such cut-throat contexts as the European horror scene and the British exploitation market.

Even so, Reeves' dedication to his mentor bordered on the obsessional. He would screen 16mm prints of Siegel's films at his house, with the neo-noir *The Killers* a particular favourite. Actor Nicky Henson recalls:

> He was always showing the bloody *Killers!* But he also had audio tapes of *The Killers.* I remember sitting there one night listening to the soundtrack of *The Killers* while having supper! (in Murray 2002: 98)

Iain Sinclair recalls appreciating the likes of *Invasion of the Body Snatchers* and *The Line-Up* (1958) but admits he had 'difficulty with the canonisation, accepting Siegel as *the* man. Mike Reeves' entire doctrine was based on that revelation' (1997: 278, emphasis in original). Indeed, Sinclair, when writing about the director's mental decline recalled how 'he had trouble sleeping and trouble talking about anything except his own problems – and Don Siegel' (1997: 296).

Given this 'canonisation', it's little wonder that a number of commentators have identified borrowings from Siegel that crop up in *Witchfinder*. Benjamin Halligan alone identifies the voice-over (inspired by a number of films including *Invasion of the Body Snatchers* and *The Duel at Silver Creek* [1952]), and the 'very, very quick cutting' (editor Howard Lanning quoted in Halligan 2003: 148), as well as suggesting that for Reeves, directing Price would have been analogous to Siegel directing Elvis in the aforementioned *Flaming Star*. It's also possible that Reeves' obsession with the American director may have been partly responsible for his problems with Price. Certainly, Siegel was fond of declaring that if a film was cast right, little direction was required: in his entertaining autobiography, 'A Siegel Film', he says of his *Riot in Cell Block 11*, 'the picture was entirely cast. No stars – just damn good actors who fit their parts' (1993: 165). Reeves seems to have felt that the option to cast right had been taken away from him by AIP and this created the oft-mentioned resentment he felt towards his star.

The similarities between Reeves and Peckinpah are made strikingly clear when one compares *Witchfinder General* and Peckinpah's *Straw Dogs*, another tale of troubled masculinity and savage violence in a bucolic English setting, photographed by *Witchfinder's* gifted cinematographer, John Coquillion. Indeed, Iain Sinclair's description of 'the stock Reevesian preoccupation: the apparently decent "normal" citizen pushed to locate the evil within himself, to absorb and reciprocate all the venom of his oppressor' (quoted in Murray 2002: 3) could apply equally to Peckinpah's film and Bissette and Winter's suggestion that *Straw Dogs* can be regarded as melding 'the American Western with the British horror film' might also be applied to *Witchfinder* (1996: 244).

As well as some obvious similarities between Siegel, Peckinpah and Reeves (such as the fact that they all made authored genre movies, often in violent action genres), there are a number of shared thematic concerns in the ouevres of all three. It goes without saying that Reeves never saw the likes of *Dirty Harry* and *Straw Dogs* and it's unclear how familiar Siegel and Peckinpah were with *Witchfinder General* (although John B. Murray is only one of a number of critics who suggest Peckinpah hired John Coquillion after watching *Witchfinder* at Siegel's behest). Rather, it's the common themes and recurring motifs in the work of all three directors that is my concern here.

VIOLENT, AMORAL PROTAGONIST

Siegel's films are full of cold, violent men with very little separating his heroes from his villains. Sometimes, his protagonists are ruthless killers (such as Lee Marvin in *The Killers* or John McBurney in *The Beguiled* [1971]) while elsewhere hero and villain are mirror images of each other. The best example of this mirroring can be found in *Dirty Harry*, arguably Siegel's best-known film, certainly his most controversial. The titular rogue cop and the psychotic hippie Scorpio are doubles of each other, both violent and racist, both dependent on the other. Eileen McGarry's comments on *Dirty Harry* also offer a perfect summation of the mirroring that occurs between Richard Marshall and Matthew Hopkins:

> the young psychotic killer is portrayed as so exceedingly debased, horrible and subhuman that he deserves to be slaughtered without consideration. (in Allison 2004)

The striking thing is that both Reeves and Seigel offer us a supremely 'killable', monstrous villain while at the same time underlining just how close Hopkins/Scorpio are to Marshall/Harry. The effect is a disturbing one and it should come as no surprise that *Witchfinder General* and *Dirty Harry* were on the receiving end of a great deal of critical opprobrium when first released.

Similarly, John Baxter's assertion that in both Siegel's 'murderers and vigilantes... he encourages us to see mirrored our own urge for violence and anarchy' (in Allison 2004) could be applied equally to Reeves' film. For Halligan, the casting of Price and the subsequent shift away from the pathetic Hopkins of the novel, led Reeves to envisage the character as the aforementioned Civil War Lee Marvin.

Peckinpah's films are full of such violent, amoral men, from the title character in *Major Dundee* (1964) and Pike Bishop in *The Wild Bunch* (1968) to Billy the Kid in *Pat Garrett and Billy the Kid* (1973) and the luckless Bennie in *Bring Me the Head of Alfredo Garcia* (1974).

'THE FOUL UNGODLINESS OF WOMANKIND'

As Siegel's films focus on *über*-masculine male protagonists, they also frequently sideline female characters. When there are strong female characters, as in his strangest film, the American Civil War gothic *The Beguiled* (regarded by both Murray and Halligan as an homage to *Witchfinder*), they tend to be jealous, repressed maids or seductive harlots who band together to murder the object of their desires. For a number of critics, his films are misogynistic: in her review of 'The Beguiled: Gothic Misogyny', Karyn Kay stated bluntly 'Don Siegel hates women – and fears them' (1976: 32).

Once again, *Dirty Harry* is emblematic in the respect. There are very few female characters who get to speak and they are all suffering: a grieving mother, the wife of a wounded cop and a terrified school bus driver. But there is an array of unclothed and/or dead women, from a swimming woman shot before the credits roll, the grotesque naked woman seen through a window, some topless dancers and the corpse of a semi-naked teenager.

However, Sam Peckinpah's reputation for misogyny easily eclipses that of Siegel: indeed, it arguably eclipses that of any other major director. Peckinpah's harsh violent films are populated with whores and faithless floozies, women who are slapped, beaten, raped and killed with a regularity that continues to alarm many critics. In *Straw Dogs*, Peckinpah set out to film 'the best rape scene that's ever been shot' (in Thomson 2002a) and the result is still troubling to many: this maddeningly ambiguous scene was the reason the film was banned on video in the UK from 1984 to 2002. There is a similar weird rape/seduction dynamic going on in Peckinpah films such as *The Getaway* (1972) and *Bring Me the Head of Alfredo Garcia* (1974) while his last film, *The Osterman Weekend* (1983) begins with a naked woman indulging in a spot of post-coital masturbation when she is killed by an injection to the face.

Certainly, *Witchfinder General* has numerous scenes of brutality to women, performed by violent male characters. But Reeves, unlike Siegel or Peckinpah, strips any ambiguity away from his sequences of violent misogyny. We are left in no doubt that Hopkins is lecherous and predatory while speaking of purity, making him not only a sadist and an accesory to murder but also a hypocrite. (Better make that in little doubt. Although it may be the work of a 'troll', the thread on *Witchfinder General*'s IMDb page, titled

'Matthew Hopkins, hero or villain?' testifies either to some ambiguity on the part of the film or stupidity on the part of some viewers.)

Peckinpah's most personal film, *Bring Me the Head of Alfredo Garcia* is another violent revenge story set in a nightmare world where the male protagonist ends up destroying himself and the woman he loves. Promoting it, the director suggested that women are 'the positive poles...the lifeforce and instinct' (Prince 1998: 149) and consequently it says much about Peckinpah's world-view that these women end up tortured, molested and killed. This is equally true of *Witchfinder*, where the 'positive poles' are slapped and hanged, poked with sticks and stabbed with spikes, burned and raped and driven mad.

CONTAGIOUS EVIL AND THE CIRCLE OF VIOLENCE

Reeves suggests an idea that was to figure intrinsically in all his features, building in prominence with each film: aggression and violence are a contaminating force, a contagion that affects everything in the vicinity. (Bill Kelley in Murray 2002: 3)

The notion of destructive evil as something that can be caught like a virus that we see in *Witchfinder General* is one that occurs in various forms in Siegel's work. In his paranoid sci-fi classic *Invasion of the Body Snatchers*, the titular aliens appear out of the sky, infecting the citizens of a small Californina town while they sleep. In *Dirty Harry*, the central character ends up little better than his nemesis Scorpio. Both men are isolated, bigoted individuals capable of extreme violence without a qualm: Scorpio laughs and jokes with the owner of a liquor store before smashing a bottle in his face while Harry shoots bank robbers while chewing his sandwich. Siegel's film portrays both men as mirror images of each other, with the only significant difference being the police badge which sanctions Harry's violence. In the climactic scene, he throws the badge away, leaving us with the uncomfortable realisation that, like Trooper Marshall, Harry has become the thing he hates most in the world.

The presence of *The Beguiled*'s soldier/killer McBurney in a girl's school serves as a catalyst for the dark desires of both students and staff, including incest, lesbianism, mutilation and murder. The Cold War thriller *Telefon* (1977) pits Charles Bronson against hapless sleeper agents who have been programmed to commit murder then suicide after they hear a Robert Frost couplet read over the telephone.

In Peckinpah's *Straw Dogs*, the central characters leave the US to escape social upheaval and unrest only to discover rape, violence and confusion in the Cornish countryside. In this strange, elliptical yet undeniably powerful film, (in)famously described by Pauline Kael as 'the first American film that is a fascist work of art' (quoted in Fine 2005: 210) violence is not something that can be shut out or avoided but a deep-seated self-destructive drive.

The cruel child: cooking potatoes in the ashes from a burning

After the witch-burning in Lavenham Square, there is a sequence where children can be seen roasting potatoes in the ashes, an image which finds a number of echoes in later Peckinpah films: *The Wild Bunch,* where children place a scorpion in an ants nest before setting it on fire or *Pat Garrett and Billy the Kid* (1973), where kids play on the town gallows, using the noose as a swing; or the children who play a part in the climactic massacres of *The Wild Bunch* and *Bring Me the Head of Alfredo Garcia.* The image of the 'cruel child' is a signifier of congenital evil.

If things had been different, *Witchfinder* and *Straw Dogs* would also share circular narratives. As the former starts and ends with screaming, the latter begins with children at play and was supposed to end with the village children, now armed for more deadly games, laying seige to the cottage. This ending would have served to further underline Peckinpah's oft-expressed belief in the violence lying dormant in everyone (even, some might say particularly, in children) and waiting for an opportunity to erupt.

But this ending was never shot, giving Peckinpah's film an odd, anti-climactic (although undeniably effective) quality. Strangely, the ending used was, like the climax of *Witchfinder*, unscripted – Dustin Hoffman improvised the last line of *Straw Dogs* as the camera rolled and Reeves and his cast and crew struggled to concoct an ending on location. After Tenser scrapped the planned climactic showdown with a band of gypsies, Reeves and Baker wrote an ending where Hopkins was burned alive before being shot by Trooper Swallow. When a demented Marshall attacks his comrade, Swallow shoots him. With the pressure on as the shoot drew to an end, the director came up with a stripped-down version of the above. Interviewed in 1999, Nicky Henson explained why:

> I said to Mike, 'We have a problem, I have got to shoot Ian.' So Mike says, 'Yeah, that's the whole point, his best friend shoots him.' I reminded him I had just used my pistol [to shoot a guard] and Mike said, 'No problem, you've got another one.' I said, 'Yeah, but I have still got to shoot Vincent, and it's not a bloody revolver.' Mike went, 'Oh Jesus'. He thought for a minute and then said he would work it out somehow. (Henson in Hamilton 1999: 53).

ANALYSIS: THE ENDING

The climactic sequence comes about after Hopkins, Stearne and their Lavenham crony, Master Webb (Godfrey James wearing an awful wig that makes him look like a seventeenth century Mo from *The Three Stooges*) have arrested Marshall and Sara on a charge of witch-craft (a blatantly false charge, even by the standards of Hopkins and Stearne).

As they leave, Hopkins is confronted by a vengeful Paul Clarke, the husband of the woman burned in the village square. Hopkins shoots him and they leave. (The unfortunate Clarke is played by composer Paul Ferris, who cuts a slightly incongruous figure with his 'anachronistically white teeth' [Sinclair 1997: 295].)

The sequence begins with the five of them walking up a hill towards the castle (in reality, Orford Castle in Suffolk). The figures and the looming castle, silhouetted against the sky, are reminiscent of the film's opening with the gibbet on the hill. Overhanging tree branches frame the image. Inside, they pass sentries as they travel down a spiral

Ending as it began, figures silhouetted against the sky.

staircase into the dimly-lit depths of the castle. The gloom of these shots offer a marked contrast with the earlier sun-lit vistas and the un-natural semi-darkness of the day-for-night scenes. In much the same way, one can't help but contrast the close-in hand-held camera work with the earlier sweeping pans and tracking shots.

Back at the lodging house, Marshall's comrades, led by Trooper Swallow, find the dying Clarke, bleeding (somewhat improbably) from the his ear, nose and mouth, a great blood stripe indicating his slide down the wall. (The colour of the blood in this scene is as phony looking as elsewhere in the film, far too bright to be real.)

In the dungeon, Marshall and Sara are tied to the wall as Hopkins heats a metal cross in a flaming brazier. Long shots reveal the claustrophobia of this bare stone room. It's as if the scale of the film has gradually shrunk, from the expansive scenery of the opening to the crowded village square in Lavenham to this subterranean chamber. Stearne jabs a metal needle into Sara's exposed back and her agonised response leaves the viewer in no doubt that this is no witchfinder's trick bodkin with a retractable point. Marshall, manacled to the wall, hauls himself up and twists around, screaming.

There is a repetition of the earlier long shot, as Swallow and his comrade approach the castle.

Hopkins heats up a cross in a brazier as Stearne and Webb untie Sara and carry her over to a stone slab where they tie her face down. (In reality, this 'torture slab' was set up to cover the well set into the castle floor.) Swallow and his companion try to convince the guard to let them pass.

The cross as instrument of torture evokes the sunshine cross in the opening shot

We see a close-up of the cross in the flames.

Swallow and his companion overpower the guard and the noise of this scuffle is heard in the chamber. Hopkins (somewhat implausibly) orders a nervous Stearne to untie Marshall so 'he can kneel before his wife and watch her suffer'. This contrivance hints at the last-minute improvisation going on during the shoot and the need to find a way for Marshall to escape.

Swallow and his companion fight another guard on the staircase. The editing in this sequence is faster-paced, moving at a Siegel-esque speed. The guard is sent tumbling down the stairs but Swallow's arm is slashed by Webb before the soldiers disarm, beat and stab him.

Stearne loses an eye

In the chamber, Marshall kicks Stearne to the ground and breaks free. In a close-up, we see Sara's pained expression. So much of the violence in this scene is channeled through

Sara, emphasising her status as what Peckinpah would refer to as 'the positive pole': we see her moaning, screaming and refusing to look, the only person not blinded by this contagious violence. From Stearne's p-o-v, we see Marshall's foot raised. He stamps on Stearne, appearing to knock out an eye. As Stearne writhes in pain, Marshall grabs an axe from the wall and sets about Hopkins. Sara screws her eyes shut tight. Eerily, Hopkins makes no sound as the blows rain down on him, the only diegetic sounds being Stearne's whining, Marshall's grunting and the sound of the axe connecting. Swallow arrives and surveys the horror of the scene: we see Hopkins in a pool of blood, Marshall still hitting him. Behind them, there is a table of iron torture implements and dark shadows thrown on the wall. Marshall's white shirt is splashed with (very red) blood. Swallow takes his comrade's gun. After saying 'May god have mercy on us all', he shoots Hopkins dead. Marshall, in close-up, half of his face masked in shadow, whispers 'You took him away from me', then louder, 'you took him from me', again and again. His voice echoes loudly in the small chamber. When he stops, Sara starts to cry as Marshall slumps to the ground, next to the twisted body of the witchfinder. As Sara's screams get louder, there is a series of shots of empty corridors and stairwells, torches flickering amidst the gloom. In one of these shots, a darting shadow can be glimpsed. The use of these shots was another instance of improvisation: they were all taken from the beginning and end of scenes shot in Orford Castle. A similar sequence of shots would be used at the end of John Carpenter's *Halloween* (1978), to express much the same thing: there is no closure and the terrible things we have witnessed can reappear anywhere. Cut back to a close-up of Sara screaming as the image freezes and the music comes in, played gently, mixing with the screams. The narrative ends up back where it began, in screams,

ineffectual prayer and a contorted lithographed face.

The last shot

VIOLENCE AS VAMPIRE BITE

The similarities between *Straw Dogs* and *Witchfinder General* manage to go beyond the visual and the thematic. The critical reaction to both films was vituperative and extreme, with a number of writers going out of their way to express displeasure. While *Witchfinder* aroused the ire of Alan Bennett, Bernard Levin and Dilys Powell, the response to Peckinpah's film was even more dramatic. Thirteen of the country's most prominent critics wrote an impassioned letter to The Times, describing the film as:

dubious in its intention, excessive in its effect and likely to contribute to the concern expressed from time to time by many critics over films which exploit the very violence they make a show of condemning. (in Petley 2002: 39)

Martin Barker's article 'Loving and Hating Straw Dogs: The Meanings of Audience Responses to a Controversial Film' (2006) attempted to identify just why it is that Peckinpah's film aroused such ire and draws on Charles Barr's piece, 'Straw Dogs, Clockwork Orange and the Critics' written for Screen in 1972. Barr was interested in the fact that a number of critics (including some signatories to The Times letter) attacked *Straw Dogs* while lauding Stanley Kubrick's *Clockwork Orange* (1972), which is, if anything, even more graphic in its portrayal of sexual violence. As Barker puts it:

Barr makes a still-compelling case that those who hated Peckinpah's film so much were expressing a fear of 'contamination' - because the film did not permit distancing from the ambiguities of feeling which the actions and events of the film portrayed. (2006)

For Julian Petley, the reaction to *Witchfinder General* was down to this same concern, the fear that, in Barr's words 'violence is a vampire bite' (1972: 26).

Many British critics have severe problems in dealing with films in which the violence is not kept comfortably remote and in which the audience, for perfectly valid and moral reasons, is encouraged to empathize with characters on screen who are caught up in violent events and situations. (Petley 2002: 37)

Whereas *Clockwork Orange* offers up a dazzling array of distancing techniques (including musical numbers, fast-motion, stylised performances and a self-conscious shooting style), Reeves and Peckinpah largely eschew such techniques. Kubrick's film is also very funny in places (with a parade of grotesques who wouldn't seem out of place in his earlier *Dr. Strangelove* [1964]) and this serves to further distance us: as James Kendrick states 'film violence is usually least enjoyable when it is taken seriously' (2009: 93). Consider how the very gory killings in later Price films such as *The Abominable Dr. Phibes* and *Theatre of Blood* are accompanied by wildly over-the-top performances, bizarre costumes and acid one-liners whereas, to recall Alan Bennett's complaint 'There are no laughs in *Witchfinder General*'.

There is also a clear desire in both *Witchfinder* and *Straw Dogs* to involve, even implicate, the viewer in the bloodshed, something which is rare in the traditional genre film (such as Hammer's gothic adventures). Tony Tenser remembered watching a screening in Southport when 'as the axe was falling, someone behind me stood up and shouted "Kill the bastard, kill the bastard! Kill the efffing bastard! Smash him! Kill him!"' (in Murray 2002: 261) and the aforementioned review by Renata Adler talks of audience members cheering the same sequence.

David Austen, reviewing an uncut print of Reeves' film before its initial release, accurately pinpointed the way that violence is used:

> The catalogue of brutality is explored in detail; at least in the prints that I have seen. I understand that the film is to be censored. In the full version the audience is spared nothing. The violence is in no way gratuitous, it is the essence of what the film is about...The bloodshed is not discreetly filmed in long-shot, it is presented as it is for the spectator to witness...But the censor, like Matthew Hopkins, has very little to do with justice. (1968: 36)

Both films present violence not as escapism or aestheticised spectacle but as contagion, a contagion so virulent that it may spread beyond the screen and infect the unwary viewer. And the director may not be immune. Defenders of Peckinpah and Reeves have stressed the moral justification in their use of violence but the truth of the matter is less cut-and-dried. Certainly, Peckinpah was no stranger to off-screen violence, much of it of his own making. And Reeves, for all his eloquently-expressed protestations to the contrary, seems to have enjoyed depicting bloodshed. Stanley Long, who shot *The Sorcerers* recalled the director's behaviour on the set:

He was flinging blood about on the set like it was going out of fashion, I mean gallons of it...it going all over the cameras and all over the crew and everybody's clothes, and I said 'Really, you know – come off it'. But he loved it. He seemed to revel in it. He definitely had a kink about blood. (in Murray 2002: 143)

Ian Ogilvy has acknowledged that, while Reeves found the 'John Wayne-sorts of bar fights wrong and immoral' in their playful violence, his primary concern was in film-making rather than pontificating: 'he was much more interested in making an exciting movie than in posing moral questions of the treatment of violence, much more' (in Murray 2002: 266).

It is worth remembering just how graphic the first drafts of the *Witchfinder* screenplay were, with scenes of soldiers being decapitated, rotting bodies and Stearne blinded and impaled.

Reeves also seems to have been interested in devising new and bloodier ways to film violent scenes. Ernest Harris, a Reeves associate, recalled the director's plans to create an opening sequence for a proposed film about a psychopathic lesbian: 'a flesh-coloured screen, an open razor slashes across seemingly cutting the screen. Blood begins to seep through and form the word the word RAZOR' (in Murray 2002: 300).

Tom Baker has also expressed some cynicism about this notion of the violence in *Witchfinder* having an overarching moral purpose. Referring to the impassioned letter Reeves wrote to John Trevelyan, Baker says:

This letter he sent from Jamaica. 'The film is violent because I am trying to put people off violence.' Ha! I can't remember if that was a heart-felt belief on his part. It may have been, but I don't remember him saying that when we were sixteen years old. [Referring to the short film *Carrion*] 'I'm screwing the bottle into the face so the people down the council estate will never be violent again!' (in Murray 2002: 256)

It's possible, even likely, that both Peckinpah and Reeves were, for all their talk of catharsis, fascinated with violence and carnage and took a certain pleasure in portraying it (in much the same way as many viewers take pleasure in watching it).

But the truth, unpalatable to some, is that violence is spectacular, revolting and yet also undeniably fascinating: why else would there be so much of it, on and off-screen?

Both directors sought to convey this paradox and this contributes to the impact of *Witchfinder General* and *Straw Dogs*, films that still retain the power to disgust, outrage and, yes, excite.

III) HE WHO FIGHTS MONSTERS...

The bleakness of *Witchfinder General* is perhaps best summed up by Frederic Nietzsche's aphorism 'He who fights monsters should look to it that he himself does not become a monster'.

Whether it was down to the war in Vietnam, the collapse of the Hollywood Production Code or the comedown from all that acid, the 'downer ending' was much in vogue in the late sixties. Think of *Bonnie & Clyde* or *The Wild Bunch* riddled with bullets, the climactic blood and flames of *Easy Rider* or Satan victorious at the end of *Rosemary's Baby* (1968). However, even in such downbeat company, *Witchfinder General* stands out.

Along with that same year's, *Night of the Living Dead* (which ends with its resourceful [black] protagonist shot by [white] rednecks, 'mistaken' for a zombie, and his body burned on a pyre), *Witchfinder General* foregrounded the nihilism, bitterness and despair that had previously only existed in the horror film as subtext. However, whereas George Romero's film is largely stripped of traditional Gothic trappings, employing the iconography of 50s sci-fi and news footage, Reeves' film does something which is perhaps more unsettling, the use of horror icon Price and the generic markers of the Hammer-esque period drama helping to make the familiar strange.

THE MOB

It's a familiar notion in gothic horror cinema, the mob of superstitious villagers turned into a motley army of peasant vigilantes, storming castles wielding flaming torches. As in the Frankenstein and Dracula cycles from Universal and Hammer, there are torch-wielding mobs in *Witchfinder General*. But rather than burning down Castle Dracula, these angry yokels set out to immolate innocent women. This depiction of the populace not as an amorphous, essentially decent, group of people but rather a baleful ignorant mass, is a disturbing one because it subverts a fundamental convention of the horror film. For Reeves, the 'monster' is not an abberation in an otherwise-ordered world; it is the world itself which is monstrous. It is as if this is Hopkins's world and Marshall and Sara are trapped in it. By the end of the film, Marshall has, in fact, succumbed to it.

This sense of unease and chaos is eloquently expressed in a number of scenes. After Marshall meets the Brandeston locals who are waiting for the witchfinder, there is a shot of one of the men, Tom Salter, a slow zoom into his blank face shadowed by the low brim of his hat. Later, the shot is repeated when Hopkins is told by one of the villagers about Stearne and Sara, the yokel's impassive face also half-obscured. There are the blank faces of the good burghers of Lavenham as they watch the witch-burning, expressing neither joy nor revulsion. As Matthew Sweet puts it 'the crowd responds not with whoops and cheers but with a strange, distracted blankness. They might be modern Britons watching the Vietnam war on TV' (2005: 270). There is no sound as they stand there, save for a baby crying. There is a certain amount of audience implication going on here, as we sit in cinemas and on sofas, watching these same atrocities with the same impassive faces. Like a number of other genre films that foreground voyeurism (such as *Peeping Tom*, *Psycho* and *Henry: Portrait of a Serial Killer* [1990]), Reeves' film sets out to create a clear identification between character and viewer. Consider the amount of times we get reaction shots of Hopkins observing torture, swimmings, hangings, burnings or the way the sensation-hungry crowds, made up not of sadists but the average, the everyday and the curious, start to disappear when the killing is over, in the opening scene and in Lavenham.

The villagers are shown as at best blank, at worst sinister

Also important is the pervasive atmosphere of malign fate which permeates the film and seems to be derived in equal measure from Thomas Hardy, John Huston and Hitchcock. Consider the way the tender scene of Marshall and Sara making love dissolves to Hopkins and Stearne. It's Marshall, after all, who gives the witchfinders directions to Brandeston. It's also Marshall's idea that Sara go to ground in Lavenham, where Hopkins and Stearne pitch up to burn witches. It's as if the events of the film are fated to happen, a series of coincidences, contrivances and chance meetings constructing an absurd nightmare world where characters cannot break free of each other.

In addition, there are a number of scenes where the editing is used to make some jarring juxtapostions, of which the dissolve from sex to the witchfinders is the most striking. Note the zoom into the fly-blown corpse of a King's man to the meat on a spit, suggesting cannibalism. After Lowes has been 'pricked' and 'ran', we see Stearne, frustrated that the torture has to stop. The scream of a drunken wench bridges the cut to the tavern, where we see him drinking and carousing, equating the sadistic drive to the sexual urge. After Sara strips and Hopkins embraces her, there is a cut to a snoring Stearne on the floor of the tavern, his hand on the breast of a topless doxy. For all his protestations to the contrary, the editing here suggests Hopkins is not so different from Stearne after all.

There is a curious number of instances where random characters pass on vital information in the form of seemingly-inconsequential remarks. Marshall hears of witch-trials in Brandeston from a horsetrader, is told that Hopkins is in Oxney by a shepherd (who spits on the ground as Marshall rides away) and later hears of the Lavenham burning from a fisherman (who is seemingly unaware that the Civil War is being fought). Stearne finds Hopkins after an exchange with another horsetrader (a very camp Wilfred Brambell who, when told that Stearne is a witchfinder answers 'that's nice. Very nice').

It's worth thinking about exactly what it is motivates Hopkins. In the source novel, there may be a lot of what Halligan calls 'cliched psychological profiles' (2003: 175) and Justin Smith describes as 'cod-psychoanalytical motivation' (2006: 93) but Bassett's Hopkins clearly believes in the existence of witches. He is also somewhat taken aback when Sara offers herself to him to spare her Uncle, unlike Price's Hopkins who obviously has designs on her from his first sighting. The Witchfinder of the film may be an enigmatic, ultimately unknowable presence but he is certainly cynical, displaying little belief in anything except power, money and lust: when told that there are three accused witches in Lavenham, two young and one old, he asks for the young pair to be sent to his room.

It may well be that the chaos of war and the resulting anarchy simply enables him to fullfil his dark desires, so he does so. There are numerous examples of this opportunistic savagery: think of the countless rapes of German women by the Red Army in the dying days of World War 2. The massacre at My Lai. The Bosnian rape camps. The torture photos from Abu Ghraib. For Justin Smith, the European witch-hunts can be seen as 'a historical period of "open season" in the physical subjugation of women' (2006: 89). As Estelle Montserrat says in *The Sorcerers*:

> We all want to do things deep down inside ourselves, things we can't allow ourselves to do. But now we have the means to do these things without fear of the consequences.

Hopkins may express his motivation, albeit obliquely. As he says, 'men sometimes have strange motives for the things they do'.

In Bassett's novel, the notion of the corrosive effects of revenge is raised by Sara in one throwaway line but in the film it is a central theme. When we first see Marshall, he may be a soldier but he's a naive and innocent one, jumpy and pale-faced when left alone after the opening skirmish with the King's men. After he kills the wounded man, Marshall appears mortified, leaving us in no doubt that he has never killed before. When he says to his Captain 'he was trying to kill you, sir' his tone is one of disbelief. The contrast between this boyish and shaken Marshall, and the climactic blood-splashed, axe-wielding one underlines the pervading air of degradation and hopelessness. There are a number of disparate films wherein an external threat turns an innocent into an avenger. As well as the aforementioned works of Mann and Peckinpah, there is the apocalyptic sci-fi of *Mad Max* (1979) and Lars Von Trier's *Dogville* (2003). There are vigilante films such as *Death Wish* (1974), *Rolling Thunder* (1977) and *Fighting Mad* (1976), advertised with the emblematic 'when you push too far, even a peaceful man gets fighting mad'. There is the rape-revenge cycle, from the glossy *Lipstick* (1976) to the grim *I Spit on Your Grave* (1978). But, unlike the traditional revenge narrative, there is precious little satisfaction gained in Marshall's drive for vengeance; just horror and madness. Perhaps only the dazzling, horrific *Irréversible* (2002) comes close to *Witchfinder's* nihilism and futility, with Gaspar Noé's Z to A narrative making it the first revenge-rape film.

Can one imagine a bleaker outlook? Evil exists in the world, not as an aberration or even as a shadow side of humanity but as a contagion that can spread like a virus and any attempt to eradicate this evil results in infection. Robin Wood has written of

> Reeves' recurrent preoccupation with the universality and the irresistible power of evil...there is again [in *Witchfinder*] the disturbing sense throughout that sanity and goodness are powerless against the all-pervading corruption and violence. (1969: 6)

Given the palpable air of toxic hopelessness that engulfs the characters in what would be the director's last film, it's easy to see why many people are still reluctant to see Reeves' death as anything other than suicide.

CHAPTER 4. THE INFLUENCE OF THE FILM

I) VIOLENCE, TORTURE AND THE DAWN OF THE SAVAGE SEVENTIES

As has been noted, both here and elsewhere, the element of *Witchfinder General* that attracted the most comment upon its initial release was the violence, specifically the graphic scenes of torture. The encouraging financial returns on the film inspired a number of direct imitations and a short-lived 'witch-craze' cycle of horror films, three examples of which will be examined in depth further on.

Witchfinder General was also one of the first of the violent films of the late sixties and early seventies. This cycle included problematic 'prestige' pictures such as *Performance*, *A Clockwork Orange* and *The Devils* as well as Hollywood films including *Dirty Harry* and *Soldier Blue* and the hard-boiled home-grown genre pieces, *Straw Dogs* and *Get Carter* (1971).

A number of these films can be linked to *Witchfinder General*. The clear connections to Siegel and Peckinpah have been explored earlier but one can also identify some common ground with *Soldier Blue*, a stomach-churning period film that sets out to evoke contemporary events (specifically, the war in Vietnam). With *Get Carter*, director Mike Hodges, like Reeves, uses graphic scenes to both rejuvenate a moribund genre (in this case, the gangster film) while at the same time attempting to de-glamourise the violence meted out.

The case of *The Devils* and a seemingly-detectable *Witchfinder* influence is an intriguing one. Director Ken Russell professed a strong dislike for *Witchfinder General*, describing it as 'one of the worst films I have ever seen and certainly the most nauseous' (quoted in Halligan 2003: 162).

However, his film, with its beautifully photographed blend of religious mania, hypocrisy, fire and torture can't help but recall Reeves' film. Particularly interesting is the jaundiced eye *The Devils* casts on the counterculture, in the form of Michael Gothard's witchfinder with his long hair and Lennon glasses. Russell's film is much more graphic than *Witchfinder*. The burning of Elizabeth Clarke pales next to the climactic immolation of Grandier and so potent is the mixture of queasy detail and sexual frankness that an uncut version of *The Devils* is yet to emerge in the UK. It is also, if anything, even more ravishing to look at: Derek Jarman's sets are some of the most striking ever seen in a British film, the black and white tiled convent, sunlight streaming through the barred windows, the piles of twisted corpses and the maggoty skeletons strapped to wheels fixed to the top of high poles. But for all its plague and vomit, stuffed crocodiles and masturbating nuns, Russell's film is ultimately a story about courage, as Oliver Reed's lusty Urbain Grandier is burned at the stake for his principled stand against the King. This stands in contrast to *Witchfinder*'s bleak circle of savagery.

II) PESSIMISM AND SOCIAL CRITIQUE

The nihilism of *Witchfinder* not only appears prescient today, anticipating the death of the 60s counterculture dream and the savagery of the 70s, but has also proven remarkably influential. British horror would get much nastier in the following decade, with the gory killings, drab settings and sleazy nihilism of Pete Walker and Norman J. Warren. Even Hammer were not immune to what one might call 'the *Witchfinder* effect'. Their *Twins of Evil* (1971), a soft-core vampire vehicle for Madeleine and Mary Collinson, the first twins to pose for Playboy, included a gang of witchfinders led by Peter Cushing. The off-beat *Demons of the Mind* (1972), meanwhile, would end, not with the studio's traditional restoration of order but abruptly with one of the main characters having a hand severed before being impaled on a burning cross. The last line of the film is 'god's will be done' and it ends on a still-image of a hysterical young woman screaming.

In Italy, Lucio Fulci, the oft-censored auteur who would go on to make a series of very gory, metaphysical horror films, directed *Beatrice Cenci* (1969). This is a Reeves-inflected story of a notorious sixteenth century Italian murder, which contains a number of graphic torture sequences and a pointed critique of the Catholic Church.

Perhaps the *Witchfinder* influence was strongest on the new wave of American horror films produced in the 1970s. Wes Craven's best films *The Last House on the Left* (1971) and *The Hills Have Eyes* (1977) both feature respectable protagonists who end up thoroughly debased by their (ambiguous) victory over the forces of sadism and chaos (a gang of grungy sex killers and a cannibal family, respectively). The climax of the celebrated *The Texas Chainsaw Massacre* (1974) also echoes Reeves' film, ending on the screams of a female protagonist driven mad by the horrors she has witnessed.

Also, a number of British horror films followed that viewed religion not as a bulwark against evil (as it was for the cross-wielding good guys of Hammer's Dracula series) but as a poisonous, destructive force for coercion and sexual repression. Think of The Brethren in *The Fiend* (1981), a glassy-eyed, whey-faced bunch of misfits getting their groove on to some (wildly-inappropriate) funky gospel. Or the murderous priest in Pete Walker's *House of Mortal Sin* (1975). Driven literally mad by celibacy, Father Meldrum strangles one victim with rosary beads, batters another to death with an incense burner and feeds another a poisoned communion wafer.

In addition, Reeves' film offered British genre filmmakers a way out of what Kim Newman has called Hammer's 'home counties Transylvania' (1988: 25) and inspired a number of horror films that reflect contemporary social concerns: the Mansonish cults of *Cry of the Banshee* (1969) and *Blood on Satan's Claw*, the clash of moralities in *The Wicker Man* (1973) and the corrupt old people who feed off the young in the work of Pete Walker (*House of Whipcord* [1974] and *Frightmare*).

This recurring motif in British horror, of predatory elders consuming (sometimes literally) the young, could be regarded as a bitter comment on the culture wars of the 1960s. For Peter Hutchings, Reeves' films demonstrate:

> an obvious lack of faith in the ability of young characters to resist the depradations of an older, repressive generation. (1993: 270)

There is certainly an eerie prescience in *Witchfinder*'s depiction of this generational struggle, with Marshall ending up every bit as monstrous as Hopkins. In much the same way, the idealism of the 'Love Generation' would spill over into violence and murder, courtesy of groups such as The Weathermen and The Symbionese Liberation Army in the US, The Angry Brigade in the UK and the West German Red Army Faction.

However, the theme of generational conflict was explored in the horror genre decades before *Witchfinder*, and since. The most familiar expression of this theme was tales of corrupted children/youth, in films as varied as *The Bad Seed* (1956), *Village of the Damned* (1960) and, later, the enormously successful demonic kid stories, *The Exorcist* (1973) and *The Omen* (1976). In the wake of the latter two box-office hits, there was a veritable kindergarten full of evil children. The disturbing *Quién puede matar a un niño/ / Would You Kill a Child?* (1976) and the better-known *Children of the Corn* (1984) and its endless sequels tell of whole communities where the young have killed off their elders.

In recent years, there's been the American films *Joshua* (2007) and *Orphan* (2009), while in the UK there are the ASBO teens of *Eden Lake* (2008) and the eponymous *The Children* (2008), victims of a virus that turns middle-class kids into parent-killing psychotics, with the memorable tag-line 'you brought them into the world, they'll take you out of it'.

Of course, a killer child is noteworthy in the same way that 'man bites dog' is. The popularity of horror films among the young also suggests a certain amount of wish-fulfillment going on. But there is another tradition, to which Reeves' film belongs, that of the old preying on the young and this theme often emerges at times of social division/ anxiety.

There are the corrupt patriarchs of German Expressionist cinema such as Drs. Caligari and Mabuse (in *Das Cabinet des Dr. Caligari* [1920]) and Fritz Lang's *Dr Mabuse* films of the 1930s). There is the character of Dracula, undying and feeding on the young and vital, whose filmed adventures tend to appear at times 'of major economic and social upheavals' (Newman 1993: 12). There are also the 'bad fathers' of *The Shining* (1980) and *The Stepfather* (1987) who represent satirical versions of the Reaganite alpha male.

Price's Witchfinder is a perfect example of this 'corrupt elder' strand and it's worth considering the fact that although the real Matthew Hopkins was a young man, there seems to have been no suggestion at any time that he would be portrayed as such. Reeves and Baker's choice, Donald Pleasance was, like Price, in his fifties when the film was made.

(III) *WITCHFINDER'S* CHILDREN

Although the thematic and stylistic concerns of *Witchfinder General* would continue to resonate through the genre for decades to come, the 'witch-craze' cycle it inspired proved less durable. The three best-known examples of this cycle can be accurately summed up (with apologies to Sergio Leone) as the good (*Blood On Satan's Claw*), the bad (*Cry of the Banshee*) and the ugly (*Mark of the Devil*).

CRY OF THE BANSHEE

Price hamming it up as Sir Edward

Gordon Hessler's 1970 film, co-written by Christopher Wicking, was another example of AIP's faux-Poe adaptations, while clearly owing much to Reeves' film. Vincent Price plays Lord Edward Whitman, decadent nobleman and witchfinder. He persecutes the cult leader Oona and her followers and in return, is stalked by a satanic werewolf (played by Patrick Mower, later to become a fixture in the soap *Emmerdale*).

Hessler and Wicking's films were of wildly variable quality. They made *The Oblong Box* (1969), which was intended as Reeves' follow-up to *Witchfinder* before he dropped out due to his deteriorating mental state. Despite a strong cast the film is distinctly underwhelming. However, their next collaboration was the far-out sci-fi/horror film *Scream and Scream Again* (1969), one of the best British horror films of the 1960s, which earned praise from, amongst others, Fritz Lang. But *Cry of the Banshee* is a mess and its many borrowings from *Witchfinder* only serve to emphasise its faults.

After an excellent opening scene animated by Terry Gilliam, with winged demons flying out of Price's head (!), Hessler's film goes rapidly downhill. It manages to be remarkably sleazy and lurid with very little actual sex but lots of exposed breasts as witches are manhandled, tavern wenches mauled and Lady Edward raped by her step-son. This, and the rickety sets, make the film look like nothing so much as 'Carry On Witchfinder'. Price's performance doesn't help matters: he is much hammier than he was in the Corman pictures. In fact this may be his worst performance, rolling his eyes and over-enunciating in an attempt to seem less bored. He seems to have set out to parody his own onscreen persona, particularly in the scene where he sees his wife's body which has turned white in her coffin and exclaims 'witchcraft'. It doesn't help that for some unfathomable reason he seems to be got up as Henry VIII in some scenes.

Early on, there is a scene of an accused witch being whipped through the village that seems to be intended as a kind of homage to/rip-off of the opening of *Witchfinder General*. But the contrast is telling. While Reeves' villagers watch all manner of atrocities blankly, without betraying the slightest emotion, Hessler's on-lookers do everything but. They yell and jeer and throw stuff and one actor really goes to town, calling out repeated variations on 'filthy witch'. David Pirie has written of the opening of *Witchfinder* how:

> the crowd who hang the witch are not blood-lusting savages but ordinary countrymen with perfectly kind faces, fascinated to watch the slaughter of an old woman. (2009: 171-2)

This creates the aforementioned uneasy identification between those watching the hanging and those of us in the cinema/on the sofa, watching the film. With *Cry of the Banshee*, no such identification is possible, as this parade of grotesques yell, chuck fruit and over-act.

The fundamental difference, however, between *Witchfinder* and *Cry of the Banshee* (and *Blood on Satan's Claw*, for that matter) is that, in the latter case(s), amidst the hysteria, torture and murder, there is a real supernatural presence. Wicking has said the character of Lord Edward was inspired by Chicago Mayor Richard Daley, who sanctioned the police brutality directed at demonstrators at the 1968 Democratic Party Convention (see Rigby 2000). The credits emphasise this attempt at social comment, with the cast divided up into The Establishment, The Witches and The Villagers. But unlike Price's Hopkins (or indeed Mayor Daley), it's hard to see Edward as a power-mad crypto-fascist when he is up against a murderous satanic avenger.

In much the same way, although the cavorting coven are very 1960s, with their hippyish dancing and incantations such as 'Oona is peace, Oona is love', they are, in turns out, in league with Satan and as such, it's hard to regard them as hapless victims of state violence, which dilutes any pretensions the film has to social comment.

BLOOD ON SATAN'S CLAW

The hippyish death cult presided over by the ironically named Angel Blake

Piers Haggard's *Blood on Satan's Claw* aka *Satan's Skin* was produced by Tigon and released in 1971. The screenwriter Robert Wynne-Simmons had originally written it as an anthology film with a Victorian setting. However, the three stories were combined and Tigon wanted the action relocated in the seventeenth century 'like *Witchfinder General*' as Wynne-Simmons recalled in 2010.[3]

There were even plans to shoot in Lavenham but the usual Tigon cost-cutting led to it being shot in an idyllic valley in Henley-on-Thames. This turned out to be a good idea, however, as the setting is an evocative one, a world away from *Cry of the Banshee*'s thatched huts and stocks built on a backlot. The *Witchfinder* influence on *Satan's Claw* is clear, with some highly atmospheric scenes of bloody horror played out against a pastoral English backdrop. Patrick Wymark even puts in an appearance, playing another patriarchal authority figure, referred to throughout simply as The Judge.

When a farmer unearths a skull (containing one wormy eyeball) in a field, it unleashes demonic forces in the local community. People start sprouting patches of black fur – 'Satan's skin' – and the village children form a witchy cult around the charismatic (and ironically-named) Angel Blake (played by 70s scream queen Linda Hayden, generating a considerable erotic charge). Like the later (and far better-known) *The Wicker Man*, Haggard's film juxtaposes pagan vitality against the puritanical forces of order. The possessed 'ecstatically nihilistic' (Hunt 2002: 94) youngsters, rebelling against their elders through sex and violence (and sexual violence) come over as nothing so much as demonic proto-hippies. Like Reeves and Baker, Haggard and Wynne-Simmons sought to comment on contemporary events through the frame of a historical setting. The brooding, apocalyptic mood of the film seems to have been shared by its young director, with Haggard writing in 1971 'I think our society is about to shatter. The whole structure is under threat for the first time' (quoted in Sweet 2005: 271).

Wynne-Simmons has acknowledged the influence of the Mary Bell case of 1968, when a 10-year-old girl killed two younger children. There are also inescapable parallels between Angel's gang and the Manson Family. Indeed, the disturbing scene where a village girl is stripped and raped while the cult members look on can be read as a grotesque parody of the orgiastic 'love-in'.

There is a striking, distinctly unwholesome eroticism to Haggard's film, a creepy kinkiness, best demonstrated when Angel buries her face in a girl's torn-off dress and later stabs her to death with shears before licking the blood off the blades. This kinkiness is there in the film's climactic showdown, as Angel is penetrated with a pitchfork and the partially-reconstructed demon is impaled on the Judge's outsized phallic cross/sword.

In some respects, the film is almost the equal of *Witchfinder,* as in the opening credit sequence set to Marc Wilkinson's atmospheric, spooky score, with the shots of a raven and skeletal tree branches against an overcast sky. Then there is the excellent cinematography by Dick Bush, full of weirdly-muted autumnal colours that make the countryside look uninvitingly cold and grim. There are a number of striking scenes, where director Haggard manages to blend the pastoral and the eerie without resorting to any obvious Reeves rip-offs, unlike Hessler and *Mark of the Devil*'s Michael Armstrong: The discovery of the skull, being pecked at by noisy crows in a freshly-ploughed field; the weird, almost blackly comic scene where a young man (Simon Williams) stabs his own possessed hand before hacking it off (and where director Haggard told Williams 'don't overact with your fingers' [see Taylor 1996]); the creepy sexiness during the climactic ritual where a woman (Yvonne Paul) strips and dances alluringly in front of a villager who has sprouted 'satan's skin', caressing a knife suggestively as she tries to seduce him into cutting off his own leg.

Like *Banshee* screenwriter Wicking, Wynne-Simmons has expressed some sympathy for his devils and some equivocation towards the Judge, saying how the demon was 'somehow more alive than the Patrick Wymark character, whose viewpoint is essentially a dead one' (in Hunt 2002: 94). The Judge is certainly a highly ambiguous figure, a cold and distant windbag of a man. He wins a game of cards against a young man with the telling line 'your elders triumph' and warns darkly that 'only the most strict discipline will save us'. The film ends on an unsettling note, with a freeze-frame of Wymark's eye amidst orange flames, an image that cannot help but recall the unearthed one-eyed skull and thus suggesting a clear link between demon and Judge.

But as with Hessler's film, any qualms one has about the methods of the Judge are tempered by the fact he is up against fur-sprouting evil teens possessed by a demon that incites them to rape and kill. When Matthew Hopkins speaks of 'the foul ungodliness of womankind' it reflects his misogyny, be it heartfelt or a calculated pose. But when the Minister in Haggard's film speaks of the 'ungodliness' of the feral village children, it's very hard to disagree with him.

MARK OF THE DEVIL / HEXEN BIS AUFS BLUT GEQÜALT

Whereas *Witchfinder General* straddles the divide between art and exploitation, the West German *Mark of the Devil* enthusiastically embraces the latter category. Its tag-lines included 'Positively the most horrifying film ever made' and 'Rated 'V' for violence'. British censor John Trevelyan refused to give it a certificate at all, while in the US it was marketed with what were euphemistically referred to as 'stomach distress bags'.

Director Michael Armstrong was regarded by some as another young auteur in the Polanski/Reeves mould but his work lacked their singular vision. Armstrong was also

One of the explicit torture scenes from Armstrong´s film

unlucky: at the age of 24, he made his first feature for Tigon, the would-be psychedelic slasher flick *The Dark*, which was supposed to star David Bowie. But the hand of the perenially-meddlesome 'Deke' Hayward led to the film being re-written, sequences re-shot and the title changed to *The Haunted House of Horror* (1969). To add insult to injury, the 30-year old American singer Frankie Avalon starred as a teenager. Armstrong's experience on *Mark of the Devil* seems to have been as bad, with extra footage being shot and inserted by the producer Adrian Hoven: the director has joked that 'there was more blood off-screen than on'.

Hoven was an actor/producer/ director (he appears in the film as the puppeteer who loses his head) whose work stretched from exploitation fare (producing Jess Franco's *Rotte Lippen Sadisterotica aka Sadist Erotica* [1968]) to the New German Cinema (with acting roles in a handful of Fassbinder films). His directorial career was less distinguished, including a soft porn version of the Siegfried legend called *Seigfried und das sagenhafte Liebesleben der Nibelungen /The Long Swift Sword of Seigfried* (1971) and a *Mark of The Devil* sequel, *Hexen geschändet und zu Tode gequalt /Mark of the Devil 2* (1973), advertised with the enticing come-on 'Ten Scenes that You Will Positively Not be Able to Stomach'!

Hoven originally wanted to direct, produce and star in what was then known as 'The Witch Hunt of Dr. Dracula', the tale of the titular vampire travelling around southern Germany in a carriage driven by an Egyptian mummy, looking for women to torture. As Armstrong tells it in an interview on the DVD release, the distributors, Gloria Films, wanted a British director and the choice was between him and Reeves 'but Mike, of course, was dead' (which must have made choosing somewhat easier).

Mark of the Devil is a strange film, an unusual blend of the atmospheric and the silly. In eighteenth century Austria, a corrupt amateur witchfinder, Albino (Reggie Nalder) is put out of a job when the renowned Lord Cumberland (Herbert Lom) arrives. Cumberland's idealistic young assistant, Christian (Udo Kier) attempts to moderate the excesses of the witch-hunt, in part to save the falsely-accused Vanessa (Olivera Katarina), who he has fallen in love with. Armstrong's film manages to be far more graphic than *Witchfinder General* without being anywhere near as harrowing. There are prickings (in close-up), branding, stretching, whippings, canings, burnings, a beheading, water torture, use of thumb-screws and a tongue pulled out. Much of the gore is too badly done to be really nasty (the tongue removal just looks ridiculous) but the whole thing has a sleazy air, only slightly leavened by the wildly-inappropriate easy-listening score. It is not entirely without merit, however. The cultish cast do their best, particularly Lom (in a bad wig) as the impotent, perhaps latently-gay Cumberland and the eerily-beautiful Kier, playing a good guy for once. Best of all is Nalder's turn as the drunk, lecherous Albino (although it's hard to see why he's called that, when he clearly doesn't suffering from albinism). The skinny, skull-faced Nalder, whose face was disfigured by burns in the 1930s in an unexplained accident, was frequently type-cast as a villain, playing an assassin in Hitchcock's remake of *The Man Who Knew Too Much* (1956) and making a terrifying vampire in the TV miniseries *Salem's Lot* (1979).

The locations, most of which were found in and around Salzburg, are striking and there is the odd memorable image, such as the weird, psychedelic light-show used to indicate when a witchfinder has been blinded by his own bodkin or the reluctant rabbit being operated as a puppet. But as with *Cry of the Banshee*, the clear borrowings from *Witchfinder* tend to demonstrate the paucity of material here. What Time Out dismissed as the 'phony Freudian motivation' (Pirie, undated) in Bassett's novel is here underlined, as Cumberland tortures and kills people he knows to be innocent due to his impotency. Armstrong claims that in his version of the film, Lom was a repressed homosexual who was in love with Christian but Hoven was uncomfortable with this and removed it. The most obvious steal from Reeves comes right at the start, when Albino sends his henchmen to attack a convoy of nuns. As one of the nuns is thrown to the ground and raped, the camera lurches to the left and we get a shot of the sun through tree branches. The bleak climax, as Cumberland escapes and Christian is executed in his place, leaving Vanessa to weep by his corpse, also feels like a Reeves rip-off, coming over as merely a sour ending rather than a devastating one.

A DIFFERENT KIND OF HERITAGE FILM?

As well as being a horror film, *Witchfinder General* is also a costume drama in a British historical setting and as such it offers a kind of 'middle way' between the 'heritage film' and the anachronistic anarchy of Peter Greenaway (*The Draughtsman's Contract* [1982]), Derek Jarman (*Carravagio* [1986], *Edward II* [1991]) and Alex Cox (*The Revenger's Tragedy* [2002]).

The heritage film evades easy definitions. The British film industry has always drawn on national history for films such as *The Private Life of Henry VIII* (1933), *That Hamilton Woman* (1941) (about Lord Nelson) and Olivier's Shakespeare adaptations *Henry V* and *Richard III* (1955) and the critic Charles Barr may have coined the phrase 'heritage film' in relation to such films; but in recent years it has become synonomous with a group of lavishly-mounted literary adaptations made in the UK in the 1980s (see Andrew Higson 1995: 2006).

This new breed of heritage films share a number of common characteristics. They are usually adapted from a 'prestige' literary source (Jane Austen, Evelyn Waugh, Charles Dickens), although a minority are based on real events (*Chariots of Fire* [1981]). They have visibly high production values, starry casts of renowned British thesps and offer up a desirable – and highly-exportable – view of national history; as Anne Morey puts it 'a kind of film tourism that reflects American expectations about a Britain ossified in a long Edwardian summer' (undated).

This 'film tourism' includes films such as *The French Lieutenant's Woman* (1981), *A Passage to India* (1984) and *A Handful of Dust* (1987) but the best-known examples of this cycle would be the films of Merchant-Ivory (the producer Ismail Merchant and director James Ivory), such as *A Room with a View* (1987), *Howard's End* (1993) and *The Remains of the Day* (1995). The responses to the work of Merchant-Ivory typify the broader response to this kind of cinema: while a number of their films were critically-acclaimed box-office hits, the vision they offered of a semi-mythical past populated by the handsome and well-to-do was seen by many as reactionary, a kind of stultifyingly tasteful nostalgia that seemed to reflect an image of Britain idealised during the Thatcher era (1979–1990). David Thomson has written of seeing *The Remains of the Day* in San Francisco, emerging from the cinema 'at three or so in the afternoon, in a throng of elderly viewers congratulating each other on how nice, how lovely, how perfect it had all been, and how "they" didn't make many films as good as that'. Thomson concludes that 'the loveliness of Merchant-Ivory gives me the creeps' (2002: 434).

But beyond the country houses of Merchant-Ivory, the heritage film is a surprisingly malleable category. Claire Monk suggests that 'part of the problem is indeed the capaciousness of the term "heritage film", coupled with the assumption that it describes a stable, unchanging genre' (2002: 7).

Witchfinder offers up a kind of twisted off-shoot of the heritage film, being based on a popular, even pulpy, novel rather than a literary work and evoking a horrific period of instability and social division rather than a desirable, highly-selective one. Not only does *Witchfinder* offer the death and destruction of war but it enthusiastically foregrounds ignorance and superstition, brutality and ugliness. Also, whereas traditional heritage films 'function as an escape from the political and social issues of the present' (Walford 2006), Reeves' film holds up a mirror to contemporary social concerns, including war, social division and generational clash.

What is striking is the unusual (although not unique) way *Witchfinder General* melds two divergent traditions, the 'respectable, highbrow' heritage film and the 'disreputable, lowbrow' horror film. There is a parallel tradition of films that react to tastefully-packaged notions of this highly-exportable British past. James Leggot has referred to this motley collection, which as well as the work of the aforementioned Greenaway and Jarman includes films by Ken Russell and even *Carry On Henry* (1971), as offering 'iconoclastic or deliberately inauthentic approaches to history' (2008: 82).

However, *Witchfinder* fits just as uneasily into this 'anti-heritage' category, offering neither avant-garde reflexivity nor parody. It also avoids overt anachronisms: the afore-mentioned nods to contemporary issues are in a different league entirely to the tuxedoes and motorbikes of *Carravaggio* or the spaceships, Nazis and giant dicks of

Lisztomania (1975). Reeves' film may be as personal as an art movie but it is clearly a popular genre film.

In his essay 'The Pattern Under the Plough', Rob Young challenges the traditional view of the heritage film, relocating it not in Thatcher-era depictions of the genteel upper-classes but rather in the 'old weird Britain' that can be found in the genre films and TV of the 1960s and 1970s. For Young, 'the great age of period drama, from the mid-1960s to mid-70s, is one of muted greens and umbers, mud, filth, grey skies and rain, where landscape is more than simply picturesque backcloth' (2010: 17).

This period encompasses a wide variety of films, from glossy prestige pictures such as *A Man For All Seasons* (1966) and *Far From the Madding Crowd* (1967), auteur works such as Russell's *Women in Love* (1969), Losey's *The Go-Between* (1971) and Kubrick's *Barry Lyndon* (1975) and horror films from Hammer and Tigon. Young's argument is persuasive and takes in not only films but TV shows such as *Arthur of the Britons* (1972) and the folk-rock of Nick Drake and Pentangle, in what he describes as 'an extremely fertile but seldom recognised moment when Britain's creative industries unconsciously examined the 'matter of Britain' (Ibid.) In addition to a brief mention of *Witchfinder*, described as being 'set in a Civil War Suffolk rendered in dirty realist style' (2010: 18), Young also brings in the Sealed Knot, a historical re-enactment society 'dedicated to recreating English Civil War skirmishes in full Cavalier and Roundhead garb' (2010: 17), a society founded, coincidentally in 1968, the year Reeves' film was released.

Perhaps the best way to place *Witchfinder General* is by turning, once again, to popular American cinema. The action genres of the Western and the gangster film can be regarded as American heritage cinema, both offering up a mythical past which is populated not by the monied upper-classes but violent men of action, pioneers and ambitious immigrants hungry for the American dream. Genres such as the Western, the gangster film or the horror film have the potential to explore the present through representations of the past. Sam Peckinpah's description of the Western as a 'universal frame within which it's possible to comment on today' (Patterson 2007) could fruitfully be applied to any popular genre.

CROMWELL AND *CROMWELL*

A number of commentators have remarked upon the omission from *Witchfinder General* of the Battle of Naseby, Tom Baker among them. Aware that 'it was very unlikely that we'd have any money for a battle' (in Murray 2002: 195) he wrote the battle scene as a montage. But as Ian Ogilvy told the same author: 'it wasn't *about* Cromwell. It wasn't about battles' (Ibid.: emphasis in original). Another contentious element is the presentation of Cromwell. Although a fine actor, the bewigged and warty Patrick Wymark is given little to do except project authority and pomposity. The fact he is gnawing on a chicken leg amuses a number of critics: Benjamin Halligan writes of 'a moment of "chicken leg" period acting – something typical for British films' (2003: 189) while the historian Alex von Tunzelmann refers to this as 'the official food of history' (2008), although she does go on to acknowledge that 'the civil war setting is accurate and evocative' (Ibid.).

Tunzelmann's fellow historian Dr. Malcolm Gaskill refers to Wymark's Cromwell as 'a dyspeptic aphorist holding court at a groaning table' before suggesting waspishly that 'Wymark, who liked a drink himself, may have thought he was playing Dr. Johnson' (undated).

Wymark's Cromwell may only appear briefly but his characterisation is unusual, in that he is portrayed neither as hero (as in Ken Hughes' *Cromwell* [1970]) or villain (Tim Roth in *To Kill A King* [2003]). These very different portayals of the character reflect an ongoing ambivalence about the man and his deeds, freedom fighter to some, regicidal proto-fascist to others. Wymark is, however, despite the reservations of von Tunzelmann, Halligan and Gaskill, a good contender for the best screen Cromwell, at least in terms of his physical resemblance. Despite his oft-quoted declaration that he should be portrayed 'warts and all', most of Cromwell's filmic incarnations have been young and considerably better-looking: Roth and Dominic West in *The Devil's Whore* (2008) are two recent examples. But the best-known depiction of the Lord Protector is that offered by Richard Harris in the aforementioned big-budget historical epic, *Cromwell*, a film which (unsurprisingly) has a number of thematic similarities to *Witchfinder*. However, despite these similarities, the two films are very different and a comparison is illuminating. *Cromwell* was directed by Ken Hughes (fresh from *Chitty Chitty Bang Bang* [1968]) and the choice of Harris is a strange one: not only is he Irish but his attempts to mask his accent are largely unsuccessful. This is a considerable irony, given the fact that Cromwell remains a figure much hated in Ireland, accused of genocidal acts against the Catholic population. It was these (still widely-disputed) war crimes that Winston Churchill referred to when he wrote how the Irish 'have used as their keenest expression of hatred "the Curse of Cromwell on you"' (1957: 9).

Hughes' film sets a glowering Harris against Alec Guiness's foppish King in a talky, lavishly-mounted spectacle. Unlike *Witchfinder General*, which utilises the pace and action of popular genres like the horror film and the Western, *Cromwell* fits comfortably into the above-mentioned category of heritage cinema. It is on an epic scale (139 minutes long and shot in 70mm), has a starry cast (including Robert Morley, Patrick Magee, a young Timothy Dalton and the ubiquitous Wymark as the Earl of Strafford), sumptuous settings and scores of extras (the battle scenes are a far cry from *Witchfinder's* skirmishes in Black Park). Hughes' treatment of the story is that of the costume epic, which had something of a resurgence in the wake of the Oscar-winning *A Man For All Seasons* but whereas the latter film is staged as a gripping drama, *Cromwell* is bogged down with exposition and is fatally uncinematic: as Vincent Canby wrote in The New York Times, the film 'presents its history which such unimaginative respect for facts... Mr. Hughes has abandoned the sort of romantic speculation that might have made Cromwell and Charles at least dramatically interesting, without substituting historical speculation that might have made them significant' (1970).

Reeves was certainly aware of Hughes' film, although he was dead by the time it was released. Ian Ogilvy recollects how the director told him:

> what we're going to do is, make a very intimate, rather nasty little story about a nasty man. But we can't do crowd scenes, Can't do them. Leave that to *Cromwell* and Richard Harris. (in Murray 2002: 195)

CONCLUSION

For every iconic British director such as Hitchcock, Michael Powell, Ken Russell or Nicolas Roeg, there is a lost talent, a figure dogged by ill health or bad luck, their filmography littered with false starts and 'what ifs?', their careers, sometimes lives, ended prematurely. This latter category includes Robert Hamer, Seth Holt and Donald Cammell. It is tempting to see Michael Reeves in a similar fashion, a promising auteur cut down in his prime, another frustrating footnote in the story of British cinema. But Reeves was more than that, being one of the handful of home-grown directors who managed to make popular cinema which is visually striking and recognisably personal. He created a fiercely-individual, albeit slim, body of work, low-budget exploitation projects which are imbued with a singular vision and culminated in *Witchfinder General*. It's a film which both adds to and comments on a number of strands in popular cinema: the gothic horror, the exploitation movie and the heritage film.

Like its near-contemporary *Performance*, another product of 1960s London, *Witchfinder General* can be seen as a mutated version of well-established home-grown genres. Just as Roeg and Cammell created a dazzling, violent blend of the gangster and pop movie traditions, so Reeves produced a film which appears to belong to a number of genres while transcending them all. Both films also pull off the rare feat of simultaneously being very much of and ahead of their time, perhaps one of the reasons why *Performance* and *Witchfinder* have undergone a torturous journey from vilification to praise. This journey is a familiar one, particularly for violent or 'problematic' films: as Steve Chibnall has said of *Get Carter* and its path from cult item to canonical text: 'clearly, the film had not changed but something in the culture of its reception had' (2008: 226-7).

Despite the indignities heaped upon it, the savage, spluttering reviews, the cutting and retitling, tampering and rescoring, Reeves' film, like many a genre monster, refuses to die. *Witchfinder General* remains a remarkable achievement, a film of great power and beauty which will, no doubt, continue to excite, move and thrill many, while (hopefully) managing to appall and distress others.

May God have mercy on us all.

FOOTNOTES

3 From Wynne-Simmons´ introduction to a screening of *Blood on Satan's Claw* at the Bloodlines Conference, De Montfort University, 5th March 2010.

BIBLIOGRAPHY

Adler, R (1968) 'Conqueror Worm: The Screamers', The New York Times
http://movies.nytimes.com/movie/review?_r=1&res=9C00E3DC1030E034BC4
D52DFBE668383679EDE (accessed November 3rd 2009)

Allison, D (2004) 'Don Siegel', Senses of Cinema.
http://archive.sensesofcinema.com/contents/directors/04/siegel.html
(accessed December 12th 2009)

anon (1968) Witchfinder General', Sight and Sound. v37:n3.

anon (1968) Witchfinder General, Variety.
http://www.variety.com/review/VE1117796427.html?categoryid=31&cs=1&query=
conqueror+worm (accessed January 2nd 2010)

Austen, D (1968) Witchfinder General', Films and Filming. v14:n10.

Barker, M (2006) 'Loving and Hating Straw Dogs: The Meanings of Audience
Responses to a Controversial Film – Part 2: Rethinking Straw Dogs as a Film',
Particip@tions Vol. 3. http://www.participations.org/volume%203/issue%201/3_01_barker.htm
(accessed December 12th 2009)

Bassett, R (1966) Witchfinder General. London: Pan Books

Benshoff, H (1997) Monsters in the Closet: Homosexuality and the Horror Film.
Manchester and New York: Manchester University Press

----- (2008) 'Vincent Price and Me: Imagining the Queer Male Diva', Camera Obscura.
http://cameraobscura.dukejournals.org/cgi/reprint/23/1_67/146.pdf
(accessed February 18th 2010)

Bissette, S and Winter, D (1996) 'Sam Peckinpah', in Newman, K (ed)
The BFI Companion to Horror. London: Cassell.

Boot, A (1999) Fragments of Fear. London: Creation Books

Brottman, M (2008) Cult Films: B Movies and Trash, Film Reference.
http://www.filmreference.com/encyclopedia/Criticism-Ideology/Cult-Films-B-
MOVIES-AND-TRASH.html (accessed 3rd March 2010)

Canby, V (1970) Cromwell, The New York Times.
http://movies.nytimes.com/movie/review?res=9E01E5DD173BEE34BC4F51D
FB667838B669EDE (accessed March 16th 2009)

Chibnall, S (2008) '*Carter* in Context' in Mathijs, E and Mendik, X (eds.) *The Cult Film Reader*. McGraw Hill Open University Press.

Churchill, W. S (1957) *A History of the English-Speaking Peoples: The Age of Revolution*. Dodd, Mead and Company: New York

Clarens, C (1971) *Horror Movies, an illustrated Survey*. London: Panther

Conrich, I (2002) 'Horrific Films and 1930s British Cinema' in Chibnall, S and Petley, J (eds.) *British Horror Cinema*. London and New York: Routledge.

Dyer, PJ (1969) *Horror Movies* review, *Sight and Sound*. v37:n7.

English Heretic (undated) 'The Curse of the Conqueror Worm' http://www.english-heretic.org.uk/ (accessed October 31st 2009)

Fine, M (2005) *Bloody Sam. The Life And Films Of Sam Peckinpah*. New York: Hyperion

Gaskill, M (undated) 'Witchfinder General', Channel Four – History. http://www.channel4.com/history/microsites/H/history/e-h/filmwitchfindergeneral.html (accessed November 7th 2009)

Halligan, B (2003) *Michael Reeves*. Manchester and New York: Manchester University Press

Hamilton, J.W (1999) 'Psychomaniac', *The Dark Side*. Issue 81

Hamilton, T (2005) *Beasts in the Cellar: The Exploitation Film Career of Tony Tenser*. London: FABPress

Hibbin, N (1959) 'Dracula's macabre decline', *The Daily Worker*, May 24th 1959

Higson, A (1995) *Waving the Flag: Constructing a National Cinema in Britain*. Oxford: Oxford University Press

------ (2006) 'Re-Presenting The National Past: Nostalgia and Pastiche in the Heritage Film' in Friedman, L.D (ed.) *Fires Were Started: British Films and Thatcherism 2nd Edition*. London and New York: Wallflower Press.

Hill, D (1958/9) 'The Face of Horror', *Sight and Sound*. v28:n1.

Horse Hospital, The (undated) 'Michael Reeves Directs – by Mark Ferreli http://www.thehorsehospital.com/archives/2007_10.html (accessed December 2009)

Hunt, L (1996) 'Witchfinder General' in Black, A (ed.) *Necronomicon Volume 1*. London: Creation Books.

------ (2002) 'Necromancy in the UK: witchcraft and the occult in British horror', in Chibnall, S and Petley, J (eds.) *British Horror Cinema*. London and New York: Routledge.

Hutchings, P (1993) *Hammer and Beyond: The British Horror Film*. Manchester and New York. Manchester University Press

Hutchinson, T (1996) 'Vincent Price', in Newman, K (ed) *The BFI Companion to Horror*. London: Cassell.

Jensen, Paul (2008 [1974]) 'Terence Fisher in conversation', *Little Shoppe of Horrors*. Issue 21.

Kay, K (1976) '*The Beguiled*: Gothic Misogyny', *Velvet Light Trap*. no 16.

Kelley, B (1991) 'Michael Reeves, Horror's James Dean', *Cinefantastique*. v22:n1

Kendrick, J (2009) *Film Violence: History, Ideology, Genre*. London and New York: Wallflower Press

Kermode, M (2002) 'The British censors and horror cinema' in Chibnall, S and Petley, J (eds.) *British Horror Cinema*. London and New York: Routledge.

Knowles, G (2007) 'Matthew Hopkins Witchfinder General' http://www.witchtrials.co.uk/matthew.html (accessed September 30th 2009)

Leggot, J (2008) *Contemporary British Cinema: From Heritage to Horror*. London and New York: Wallflower Press

Lucas, T (2009) 'Still Casting a Spell', *Sight and Sound*. v19:n6

Malcolm, D (2000) *Witchfinder General, The Guardian*. http://film.guardian.co.uk/Century_Of_Films/Story/0,,408045,00.html (accessed October 21st 2009)

Milne, T (1968) '*Witchfinder General*', *Monthly Film Bulletin*. v35:n413

Monk, C (2002) 'The Heritage Film and Gendered Spectatorship', Close Up, The Electronic Journal of British Cinema. http://www.shu.ac.uk/services/lc/closeup/monk.htm (accessed February 10th 2010)

Morey, A (undated) 'New Understandings of the Heritage Film', *Film Reference*: Heritage Films. http://www.filmreference.com/encyclopedia/Criticism-Ideology/Heritage-Films-NEW-UNDERSTANDINGS-OFTHE-HERITAGE-FILM.html (accessed February 10th 2010)

Murray, John B. (2002) The Remarkable Michael Reeves. London: Cinematics

N, D (2007) 'What if? Michael Reeves' *We Can Rebuild Him*.
    http://onedeadfish.blogspot.com/2007/05/what-if-michael-reeves.html
    (accessed November 3rd 2009)

Newman, K (1988) *Nightmare Movies, A Critical Guide to Contemporary Horror Cinema*.
    New York: Harmony Books

----- (1993) 'Bloodlines', *Sight and Sound*. v3: n1

----- (2003) DVD notes, *Witchfinder General* Prism DVD

Patterson, J (2007) 'Whatever Happened to the Heroes?', *The Guardian*
    http://www.guardian.co.uk/film/2007/nov/16/2 (accessed December 27th 2010)

Petley, J (1986) 'The Lost Continent' in Barr, C (ed) *All Our Yesterdays. 90 Years of British Cinema*.
    London: BFI

----- (2002) "A crude sort of entertainment for a crude sort of audience': the   British critics
    and horror cinema' in Chibnall, S and Petley, J (eds.) *British Horror Cinema*. London and New
    York: Routledge.

Pirie, D (2009) *A New Heritage of Horror*. London and New York: I.B. Tauris

----- (undated) *Witchfinder General, Time Out*.
    http://www.timeout.com/film/reviews/64697/Witchfinder_General.html
    (accessed January 2nd 2010)

Prince, S (1998) *Sam Peckinpah and the Rise of Ultraviolent Movies*. University of Texas Press

Rayns, T (2006) 'What might have been' in *Time Out 1000 Films to change your life*.
    London: Time Out Guides.

Rigby, J (2000) *English Gothic*. London: Reynolds and Hearn

Robertson, J.C (1993) *The Hidden Cinema: British Film Censorship in Action 1913–1975*. London:
    Routledge

Sandford, C (2007) *Roman Polanski*. London: Century

Sarris, A (undated) 'Don Siegel', *They Shoot Pictures, Don't They?*
    http://www.theyshootpictures.com/siegeldon.htm (accessed November 1st 2009)

Siegel, D (1993) *A Siegel Film*. London and Boston: Faber and Faber

Sinclair, I (1997) *Lights Out for the Territory*. London: Granta Books

Smith, J (2006) *Cult Films and Film Cults in British Cinema*. University of Portsmouth: PHD Thesis

Sweet, M (2005) *Shepperton Babylon*. London: Faber and Faber

Taylor, D (1996) Don't Overact with your Fingers! The Making of *Blood on Satan's Claw* in
    Jaworzyn, S (ed.) *Shock! The Essential Guide to Exploitation Cinema*. London: Titan

Thomson, D (2002a) 'Film Studies: Paranoid and violent -Peckinpah comes back to haunt us',
    The Independent, http://www.independent.co.uk/arts-entertainment/films/features/film-
    studies-paranoid-and-violent--peckinpah-comes-back-to-haunt-us-644113.html
    (accessed October 2008)

----- (2002b) *The New Biographical Dictionary of Film: 4th Edition*. London: Little, Brown

----- (2004) 'Film Studies: Dark, depressive, volatile – the film buff who lost the plot',
    The Independent, 11th July.

Trevelyan, J (1973) *What the Censor Saw*. London: Michael Joseph

von Tunzelmann, A (2008) 'Reel History: Where Was Vinegar Tom?', *The Guardian*
    http://www.guardian.co.uk/film/2008/sep/25/1 (accessed October 17th 2009)

Walford, M (2006) 'The Heritage Film in British Cinema Part 1', *Kinoeye*.
    http://blogs.warwick.ac.uk/michaelwalford/entry/open_studies_in_1_2_3_4_5_6_7_8_9_245/
    (accessed February 10th 2010)

Watkins, P (2009) 'Culloden', *Peter Watkins*.
    http://pwatkins.mnsi.net/culloden.htm (accessed November 20th 2009)

Williams, L.C (1995) *The Complete Films of Vincent Price*. New York: Citadel Press

Wood, R (undated) 'Anthony Mann', *Film Reference*.
    http://www.filmreference.com/Directors-Lu-Mi/Mann-Anthony.html
    (accessed November 21st 2009)

----- (1969) 'In Memoriam Michael Reeves', *Movie*. Winter 1969 – 70.

Young, R (2010) 'The Pattern Under the Plough', *Sight and Sound*. v20: n8.

Beyond Hammer

British Horror Cinema Since 1970

James Rose

Devil's Advocates

"Auteur Publishing's new Devil's Advocates critiques on individual titles offer bracingly fresh perspectives from passionate writers. The series will perfectly complement the BFI archive volumes." Christopher Fowler, Independent on Sunday

Let the Right One In — Anne Billson

"Anne Billson offers an accessible, lively but thoughtful take on the '80s-set Swedish vampire belter... a fun, stimulating exploration of a modern masterpiece." Empire

Witchfinder General — Ian Cooper

"I enjoyed it very much; it sets out all the various influences, both before and after the film, and indeed the essence of the film itself, very well indeed." Jonathan Rigby, author of English Gothic

Saw — Benjamin Poole

"This is a great addition to a series of books that are starting to become compulsory for horror fans. It will also help you to appreciate just what an original and amazing experience the original SAW truly was." The Dark Side

The Texas Chain Saw Massacre — James Rose

"[James Rose] find[s] new and unusual perspectives with which to address [the] censor-baiting material. Unsurprisingly, the effect... is to send the reader back to the films... watch the films, read these Devil's Advocate analyses of them." Crime Time

Printed and bound by CPI Group (UK) Ltd, Croydon, CR0 4YY

25/03/2025

14647350-0002